Essential Writings of Karl Marx

Hank Duncan
Spring 1976

Sharon Krueger

590/-

Other Books by David Caute

Essential Writings of Karl Marx

Selected, and with an Introduction and Notes, by

David Caute

 COLLIER BOOKS, NEW YORK, NEW YORK

The Macmillan Company
866 Third Avenue, New York, N.Y. 10022
Library of Congress Catalog Card Number: 68-21364
Originally published in Great Britain in 1967 by MacGibbon &
Kee Limited, London
First American Edition published in a hardcover edition by
The Macmillan Company in 1968
First Collier Books Edition 1970
Second Printing 1971
Printed in the United States of America

Contents

Editor's Note

The editions from which the extracts published in this book are drawn are listed below.

Acknowledgment is due to Messrs. Lawrence and Wishart Ltd., and to Messrs. C. A. Watts & Co. Ltd., for permission to quote from translations under copyright.

The following abbreviations have been used in the references.

C.I.   *Capital*, Volume I, (1867).
        Translated by Samuel Moore and Edward Aveling, edited by F. Engels. London, Lawrence & Wishart, 1961.

C.III. *Capital*, Volume III, (1894).
        Edited by F. Engels. Translated with reference to the translation published by Charles H. Kerr & Co., Chicago. London, Lawrence & Wishart, 1962

C.M.   *Manifesto of the Communist Party* (1848). Translated by Samuel Moore, Moscow, Foreign Languages Publishing House, n.d.

E.P.M. *Economic and Philosophic Manuscripts of 1844* (1844). Translated by Martin Milligan, London, Lawrence & Wishart, 1961.

E.W.   *Karl Marx, Early Writings*. Translated and Edited by T. B. Bottomore, London, C. A. Watts & Co. Ltd., 1963.
        'Bruno Bauer, "Die Judenfrage"', 1843. 'Contribution to the Critique of Hegel's Philosophy of Right', 1844.

G.I.   *The German Ideology* (1846). Edited by R. Pascal, New York, International Publishers Co. Inc., 1947. New World Paperback Edition, 1963. London, Lawrence & Wishart.

H.F.   *The Holy Family* (1845). London, Lawrence & Wishart, 1956.

O.R.   *On Religion*. London, Lawrence & Wishart, n.d.
        'The Communism of the Paper *Rheinischer Beobachter*'.

P–C.E.F. *Pre-Capitalist Economic Formations* (1857–8). Translated by Jack Cohen. Edited by Eric Hobsbawm, London, Lawrence & Wishart, 1964.

P.P.   *The Poverty of Philosophy* (1847). London, Lawrence & Wishart, n.d.

S.C.   *Marx-Engels Selected Correspondence*, London, Lawrence & Wishart, 1956.

S.W.I. *Karl Marx and Frederick Engels, Selected Works*, Volume I. London, Lawrence & Wishart, 1962.
        'Wage Labour and Capital' (1847).
        'The Bourgeoisie and the Counter-Revolution' (1848).

'Address of the Central Committee of the Communist League' (1850).

'The Class Struggles in France, 1848–1850' (1850).

'The Eighteenth Brumaire of Louis Bonaparte' (1851–2).

'Preface to *A Contribution to the Critique of Political Economy*' (1859).

'Inaugural Address of the Working Men's International Association' (1864).

'Wages, Price and Profit' (1865).

'The Civil War in France' (1871).

S.W.II. *Karl Marx and Frederick Engels, Selected Works*, Volume II, London, Lawrence & Wishart, 1962.

'Critique of the Gotha Programme' (1875).

The editor of this volume, David Caute, was born in 1936. He studied Modern History at Wadham College, Oxford, and was a Fellow of All Souls College from 1959 until 1965. He is currently a Visiting Professor at New York University.

Introduction

The present collection of selected writings is designed to provide a general introduction to Marx's work as a whole. The texts have been set out in a way which indicates not only how Marx's ideas developed in the course of his lifetime, but also how they are related to one another as components of his general system. It is one of the great merits of Marx that his thought cannot be broken down simply into 'history', 'philosophy', 'economics' and 'politics'. Marxism is a unity. But its internal logic requires us to begin with Marx's debt to and rebellion against the philosopher Hegel. From this philosophy flowed a view of man as an alienated and degraded being, a creature in the grip of blind greed, no longer master of his own fate, organised in mutually antagonistic classes and perpetually at war with his fellow men. The whole body of thought we call Marxism is founded on this vision of contemporary man, and on the conviction that this appalling condition not only can be, but inevitably will be destroyed and surpassed by social action.

Marx related the consciousness of men, their ideas and beliefs, to their situation in society. Mid-nineteenth century society he defined as 'capitalism'. Convinced that capitalism represented the ultimate and most extreme form of class rule and economic exploitation, he devoted much of his life to a detailed study of its mechanisms and what he regarded as its inherent and self-destructive defects. He attempted to demonstrate how government, the state, generally reflected the power and interests of the dominant class, and how the overthrow of capitalism required the violent, revolutionary overthrow of the capitalist state. But he was not content to describe and predict. For Marx thought and action were inseparable. More than once in his life he attempted to organize a revolutionary workers' movement, to destroy the old order in Europe, and to bring about the rule of the universal class of the future, the proletariat. Always he was sustained in his efforts by the vision of an ultimate communism in which men would recover their true nature and live in perfect harmony.

The reader will no doubt form his own judgments and impressions from the texts themselves. The commentary and notes which I have provided are intended to clarify some points and to make connections between others. I have not attempted to be uncritical or aspired to be 'impartial'. Marx himself would have ridiculed the idea of an 'impartial' evaluation of his own work. Marxism claims to be a science of society, but it is also unashamedly partisan. It insists – as we shall see later – that a social science *must* be partisan. Marx's philosophy is a total philosophy in the sense that it purports to provide a general sociological analysis of the past, present and future. To be 'open-minded' in the face of such a philosophy would simply to be empty-headed. All our preconceptions and preferences are immediately involved, whether we like it or not. Of course there are certain standards of objectivity which can and must be observed. Too many writers have twisted facts and distorted what Marx actually said in order to support their friendly or unfriendly image of him. Many of them have written under external pressure, to serve a political party or to use Marx one way or another as a weapon in the Cold War. I hope to have avoided these pitfalls. But I do not claim to be impartial, and I certainly do not suggest that my own view of what has happened in East and West since Marx's death in 1883 has not affected my opinion of Marx himself.

Marx's lifelong friend and collaborator was Friedrich Engels. Generally they were in agreement. Indeed, the most readily accessible and easily readable general survey of the Marxist position was written by Engels (*Anti-Dühring*). But for reasons of space I have quoted from Marx alone. He was undoubtedly the more original, subtle and profound thinker of the two, and it is in any case by no means certain that he would have endorsed everything that Engels wrote during the prolific last years of his life. (Engels outlasted Marx by thirteen years.) It is Marx who continues to fascinate us to an extraordinary degree. Like Aristotle in the later middle ages, he remains a unique point of reference, a gigantic intellect, an undoubted genius whom no one concerned about the world in which we live can safely ignore.

Karl Marx was born in 1818. His parents were Rhineland Jews who had been converted to Protestantism. Marx himself was baptised at the age of six. His father, Heinrich Marx, was a lawyer who had absorbed the ideas of Voltaire, Rousseau and of the 18th century rationalists in general – ideas which he readily communicated to the young Marx.

As a student, first at Bonn then at Berlin, Marx revealed literary aspirations as well as talents as a philosopher. But after he had earned a doctoral degree on the basis of a thesis on the Greek philosophers Democritus and Epicurus, it was towards political journalism rather than poetry that he turned. He and the other 'Young Hegelians' whom he had met in Berlin were agreed that philosophy must achieve its ends, must realize itself, in the sphere of politics and in the reform of the state.

Spurred on by a Prussian royal instruction of 1841 which reinforced the censorship system, Marx began to publish highly critical articles in a number of reviews. In 1842 he was appointed editor of the democratic newspaper, *Die Rheinische Zeitung*, published at Cologne. The paper was suppressed in January 1843.

When Marx moved to Paris in October of that year, he was not yet a fully-fledged 'Marxist'. His attitude towards communism was still equivocal, and his conception of the proletariat abstract and philosophical. But Paris in the 1840's was seething with unrest and practical socialist activity; here were to be found Louis Blanc, Proudhon, the followers of Blanqui, Weitling and Flora Tristan – reformers and revolutionaries who knew of the working class at first hand and who aspired to overthrow capitalist society with their hands as well as their heads. Marx was deeply impressed; by the end of 1844 his ideas had matured. But Europe was not at this time an easy place for revolutionaries. A series of anti-Prussian articles which he published in a German emigré magazine brought protests from the Prussian government and Marx's expulsion from France by Guizot. He moved to Brussels and resumed his revolutionary and literary activity. *The Holy Family*, written in Paris, was published in 1845, but the more important *German Ideology*, also written in collaboration with Engels, failed to find a publisher during its authors' lifetime.

Engels had already embarked on his reluctant career as a

capitalist in the family firm in Manchester. It was in 1844–5 that his friendship and intellectual collaboration with Marx, which was to endure until Marx's death, took positive shape.

In Brussels Marx joined the League of Communists and became Vice-President of the Brussels Democratic Association. In 1847 he and Engels were commissioned by the League to write what turned out to be the most famous document of revolutionary communism – *The Communist Manifesto*. The *Manifesto* was published early in 1848, just as a wave of revolution broke across the length and breadth of Europe; in the turmoil it passed almost unnoticed.

In April 1848 Marx and Engels returned to Germany to pitch themselves into the struggle. Marx got himself appointed editor of *Die Neue Rheinische Zeitung*, a bourgeois-democratic paper and a successor to the old *Rheinische Zeitung*. Under Marx's guidance the paper called for a single, democratic German Republic and a revolutionary war against Tsarist Russia in the name of a free Poland. But elsewhere Marx urged the German workers to form their own independent organizations and on no account to surrender their arms to the bourgeois democrats. Marx, in fact, was preparing for 'permanent revolution'.

It never came. Throughout Europe the counter-revolution triumphed. Marx himself was arrested, charged with sedition, and then acquitted in February 1849 at the famous Cologne trial. Expelled from Germany, he returned to Paris, but after the demonstrations of February 1849 he was forbidden to remain there and so he withdrew to London, where he remained for the rest of his life.

The initial effect of defeat was to strengthen Marx's ties with the violently revolutionary followers of Auguste Blanqui within the Universal Society of Revolutionary Communists. But the comrades soon fell out. Marx declared the Society dissolved and gave warning that the revolution would require a long period of preparation and propaganda among the European workers. The League of Communists also broke into rival factions, leaving a legacy of bitterness and recriminations among the German emigrés.

It was at this period that Marx wrote his brilliant accounts of the events of 1848–51 in France, *The Class Struggles in France* and *The Eighteenth Brumaire of Louis Bonaparte*. Very poor now, he attempted to keep his family alive by journalism. He wrote regular articles, often with the help of Engels, for the *New York Tribune*. In the British Museum he embarked upon the immense research, the empirical investigations of English conditions, which were to culminate in his master work, *Capital*. But during these years he was dogged by poverty, illness, humiliation, family tragedy and the loneliness of exile. His works were proscribed and confiscated in Germany. It was only periodic gifts of money from Engels in Manchester which kept him from complete ruin and an early grave.

The publication of the first volume of *Das Kapital* in Germany in 1867 had been foreshadowed by an important earlier work, *A Contribution to the Critique of Political Economy (1859)*. Neither work drew much attention, critical or otherwise; indeed Engels was forced to write a number of reviews of *Capital* himself, some of them anonymous.

From 1863 until 1872 Marx's sense of frustration was lessened by a welcome opportunity to throw himself once more into the active political struggle. The International Working Men's Association – the First International – was founded in 1864 on the basis of an agreement between certain French and English trade union leaders. Although the International failed to gain wide support in Germany, Marx, through tact and persistence, managed to bring the General Council in London under his own ideological influence and to advance his views at international Congresses at the expense of rival socialist schools, particularly the followers of P.-J. Proudhon. But after the defeat of the Paris Commune in 1871 Marx and Engels could no longer maintain control of the International, which was about to fall under the control of the heroic Russian anarchist, Bakunin.

Marx's last years saw some alleviation of his financial position, but he was practically burnt-out at the age of fifty. It was now Engels, who had retired from business, who took up and completed the projects which Marx would have liked to have undertaken. Marx never completed the last two volumes of *Capital*, which Engels put together from voluminous notes after his death.

Although Marx bitterly criticised the programme adopted by the founding Congress of the German Social Democratic Party in 1875, in which he detected too much of the influence of his rival Lassalle, he did at least have the satisfaction of witnessing the core of his own ideas taking root among the German working class. But when Marx died in 1883 the Social Democratic Party was still suffering under Bismarck's anti-socialist laws. It was Engels who lived to see the Party develop into a mass movement, the most powerful in Europe.

Marx's general system is sometimes described as 'dialectical materialism' and sometimes as 'historical materialism'. (Marx himself did not use either term, although he did refer to his own 'dialectical method' and its 'historical base'. The terms were in fact first employed by Engels and the Russian Marxist, Plekhanov). Soviet Marxists have followed the distinction used by Engels: dialectical materialism describes the system as a whole, in its application to history, society *and the natural sciences*. Historical materialism therefore means the application of the general system to human history. But this presents one major difficulty.

Does a dialectical analysis of inanimate nature – a dialectical physics, chemistry or geology – have any meaning? Engels (see his *Dialectics of Nature*) thought that it did; and he also said that Marx agreed. In Engels' opinion, Marx had failed to elaborate a dialectics of nature only through practical considerations – absorbed by his economic studies and constantly ill, he had found insufficient time to keep up with the natural sciences. This may or may not be. It can readily be argued that Engels in his last years shed the Hegelian and exaggerated the positivist trends in Marx's thought. Although Marx had given Hegel's dialectic a materialist basis, the element of *mind, intention and consciousness* remained an integral and indispensable causal factor in his writings. Marx's system has meaning only in so far as it describes the interpenetration of the whole and the parts, of men, classes and social structures, in the *human* world. In fact, Engels' 'three laws' of dialectics are now generally regarded as self-defeatingly schematic. The relevance of the dialectic – whether regarded as an immanent law of development or as a method of understanding that development – to the natural sciences appears unproven (although scholars disagree about this). I shall therefore employ the term 'dialectical materialism' throughout as identical with historical materialism.

Marx was a materialist – or he became one. What does this mean? It certainly does not mean someone whose only gods are material greed and gain, and who is contemptuous of all ethical or aesthetic values. (Paradoxically, many politicians who today like to denounce 'materialism' proclaim in the same breath that the profit motive alone can generate a productive economy). As a technical term, materialism suggests a view of reality and of causation. It recognises not only that the world exists (a proposition many times challenged!) and is composed of physical matter, but it also claims the primacy of matter over mind.* Materialists deny the existence of any God or Idea or Absolute Spirit which is prior to the material world and which can account for its development. On the contrary, they prefer to explain gods, spirits and ideas as reflections of, or rationalisations of, or failures to understand fully the material world itself. Marx inherited his materialism partly from a French and English tradition of the 17th and 18th centuries, and more immediately from his fellow-German contemporary, Ludwig Feuerbach. Marx's notable and distinctive contribution to philosophy (and to history and sociology) was to have interpreted material evolution in the human world in terms of a dialectical movement, and also to have located the decisive material factor as the economic factor, the forces of production and the class relationships which these forces engender. Marx said that all previous history was the history of class struggles. No one had put it quite that way before.

Marx like Hegel depicted human society as being in a state of constant dialectical movement. But whereas with Darwin evolution is not finite and does not presuppose either a beginning or an end, with Hegel and Marx there is an end, a condition towards which society is progressing, a condition of complete harmony and integration in which man will rediscover his true, fulfilled nature. Marx called this society communism. Like Hegel, he saw in the historical process a principle of necessity. Each determinate state of Being is viewed against an ultimate Essence, which suggests the unity of Being throughout change. In an important sense this Essence is linked to the ultimate stage when the potential will have become the actual, and when the

---

* Here it should be added that materialists differ among themselves as to how precisely matter inflicts itself on mind, and what 'mind' in fact is.

real and the rational will once again be identical. Man becomes himself. The dichotomy of 'is' and 'ought' is resolved. Marx shared with Hegel the urge to incorporate all life, history and culture into a unitary scheme in which man would finally be at one with himself. Thus although at first sight Marx, with his stress on conflict, on revolution, on the overthrow of one society by a succeeding one, might seem to be the enemy of all conservatism, it has to be remembered that he was talking only about the childhood of civilized society, about what he called 'pre-history'.

This ideal undoubtedly springs from a view of man's true or ultimate nature. 'What is the kernel of evil?' Marx wrote in his notes. 'That the individual locks himself in his empirical nature against his eternal nature.' The whole notion of alienation or estrangement, which Marx adapted from Hegel, implies an original human nature to which it is man's historical mission finally to return.

Marx's revolt against the society in which he lived was clearly an ethical revolt. But he was no more prepared than Hegel to assign ethics and reason to separate compartments. Marx did not say that capitalism is bad and communism good; he preferred to argue that class society distorts and degrades man, that it is 'inhuman' in the sense that it warps the personality. It is therefore irrational. Later in the 19th century a number of socialist theorists, notably Eduard Bernstein, insisted on disentangling ethics and dialectics and rejected the notion that morality was *immanent* in the historical process. This revisionist tendency generally went hand in hand with practical reformism and a willingness to compromise with capitalism. This may partly be due to the fact that recognition of ethics as an autonomous sphere compels a consideration of means as measurable against ends. Violence, it is argued, does more harm than good. Compromise is the only solution.

Marx and Engels were wary of exposing their moral feelings. But moral indignation is implicit in much of what they wrote. *Capital*, which includes detailed descriptions of working-class poverty, ignorance, disease, degradation and death, vibrates with indignation.

One of the most interesting features of Marxism is its distinction between superstructure and infrastructure, between laws, ideas, moral codes, political organisms on the one hand, and the forces of production on the other. Marx regarded the economic factor as being ultimately determinant in history. The problem is *'how ultimately'*? Marx himself insisted that men make their own history; they make the choices and decisions, it is they who are capable of courage or cowardice, wisdom or folly. But an even more basic difficulty arises. Is a distinction between superstructure and infrastructure wholly possible? Soil, climate and mineral resources are admittedly purely 'material' factors. But even the simplest tool is made by man and is a product of his intelligence and his intentions. Technological innovations, the transition from hand-mill to steam-mill, from workshop to factory, cannot be regarded as purely material progress. Marx seems to have arbitrarily removed common sense and even science from the superstructure, which he confined to such constantly changing entities as law, customs, forms of government and religious beliefs. But can laws and beliefs be logically separated from the more permanent categories of thought and language of which they are comprised? And if these more permanent categories cannot, as we have seen, logically be separated from material or economic life, then is the general distinction between superstructure and infrastructure a useful one?

The same problem applies to the question of consciousness. Marx said that life determines consciousness. But what is 'life' apart from consciousness?

A key to Marx's pattern of thought in this respect is to be found in his notion of 'false consciousness'. False consciousness is a distorted mental picture of reality, and its source is the alienation of man in class society. Alienated man no longer understands the world for what it is; he feels estranged from and powerless over the products of his own hands. Divided against his fellow men, he becomes the victim of passion and greed. False consciousness is the source of ideology, of generalised dogmas in class society. It is ideology in this sense which Marx assigns to the superstructure, and which he explains in terms of prevailing economic forces and economic relations. In the future communist society the distinction between superstructure and infrastructure would automatically disappear. Ideology would disappear; man would be guided by pure reason.

The proposition that life determines consciousness assumes

an added ambiguity when we study Marx's career as an active revolutionary, or the history of subsequent Marxist political movements. Taken as a whole, Marx's writings would suggest that the predicament of the modern proletariat, its increasing poverty, its merciless exploitation by the bourgeoisie, its lack of property and its lack of illusions must in the end generate class consciousness and the will to revolutionary action. A central theme of *The Communist Manifesto* is the gradual and inexorable growth and impoverishment of the proletariat until a situation is reached in which revolution follows almost automatically.

On the other hand, we find Marx complaining in the 1860's that although England was ripe for revolution, the English workers lacked revolutionary ardour. Evidently the 'situation' did not generate the expected consciousness on all occasions. Nor did Marx expect it to. In the 1840's he had made much of the point that theory and philosophy – scientific socialism – become in the final struggle vital weapons in the proletarian armoury. At the moment of its triumph the working class must be conscious of its historical role. Throughout his life Marx fought an uphill battle to get the working-class movements of England, Germany, France and other European countries to banish their reformist inhibitions, to reject false prophets like Proudhon and Lassalle, and to accept and act upon the tenets of scientific socialism. In what sense, then, does life determine consciousness?

Lenin stated the problem with brutal simplicity. If left to itself, the working class was incapable of transcending a negative, trade-union consciousness, a narrow obsession with short-term reforms and immediate gains. A true revolutionary attitude, a political consciousness, could only come from outside the proletariat. Hence Lenin's excessive stress on correct theory, on the party and on the activities of professional revolutionaries. In some present-day Marxist circles Lenin's emphasis has been magnified to the point where it is argued that all that now stands between the West European proletariat and a socialist revolution is a lack of sound doctrine and dynamic leadership.

But the truth of the matter is that capitalism has not followed the downward, suicidal course predicted by Marx. At least for the time being, capitalism has learned lessons, adapted itself and survived. Perhaps this is because capitalists do possess what

Marx denied to them – an element of free will and the ability to make short-term sacrifices in order to guarantee long-term profits.

Marx's analysis of capitalism, its laws and its future tendencies are set out, with editorial comments, in a later section of this book. Marx was a self-taught economist and a very competent one. He laid bare many myths which had been advanced by the English classical economists and readily accepted by a bourgeoisie for whom *laissez-faire* was a law of life, the only sound principle of economic prosperity. Unfortunately he went in for long-term predictions on a massive scale. Of course, many modern economists indulge in predictions – governments employ them to do so. But Marx's predictions were of a different order and were undoubtedly spawned by the general historical and sociological conceptions which he had acquired in the 1840's, before he undertook his detailed, empirical investigation of contemporary capitalism. He remained throughout his life an Hegelian. His *overall* vision of history, his abiding certainty that an imperfect and irrational society was a transitory phase leading to a completely rational, harmonious and integrated world – this was the vision which drove him to convince himself that capitalism must imminently annihilate itself by breeding the agent of its own destruction, the proletariat. His entire analysis of the future of capitalism is moulded in conformity with this vision.

Naturally this factor detracts from our estimation of Marx as an economist. It is equally a fault in his philosophy. No science has yet been evolved which permits us to describe the future in the way that Marx sketched out the principles of life under socialism and mature communism. The dialectic gives no more validity to prediction than do other ways of regarding reality; it is not a crystal ball. Hegel had claimed that human history was reaching ultimate fulfilment in his own country under his own eyes. Marx claimed that history was on the very verge of substituting the realm of freedom for the realm of necessity. Like Hegel, he was a prophet. He was equally a fighter, a champion of the working class. But he was also a great scholar, a historian of enormous erudition, a pioneer of modern sociological analysis. For this reason Marx and Marxism remain elusive.

PART ONE

Foundations of Marxism

A. The Philosophical Heritage

[In this passage, published in 1845, Marx surveys and passes judgment on his own philosophical inheritance. His analysis sweeps over the whole rationalist and materialist tradition from Thomas Hobbes in the 17th century to the 'utopian' socialists Owen, Fourier and Cabet, who were Marx's contemporaries. Marx was himself a materialist and opposed to all metaphysics. However, it can be argued that the dialectical method which he inherited from Hegel is in fact a metaphysical one.]

'Speaking *exactly* and in the *prosaic* sense,' the French Enlightenment of the eighteenth century, in particular *French materialism*, was not only a struggle against the existing political institutions and the existing religion and theology; it was just as much an *open* struggle against *metaphysics* of the *seventeenth century*, and against all metaphysics, in particular that of *Descartes, Malebranche, Spinoza and Leibnitz. Philosophy* was opposed to *metaphysics* as *Feuerbach*, in his first decisive attack on *Hegel* opposed *sober philosophy* to *drunken speculation.* Seventeenth-century *metaphysics*, beaten off the field by the French Enlightenment, to be precise, by *French materialism* of the eighteenth century, was given a *victorious and solid restoration* in *German philosophy*, particularly in *speculative German philosophy* of the nineteenth century. After *Hegel* linked it in so masterly a fashion with all subsequent metaphysics and with German idealism and founded a metaphysical universal kingdom, the attack on *speculative metaphysics* and *metaphysics in general* again corresponded, as in the eighteenth century, to the attack on theology. It will be defeated for ever by *materialism* which has now been perfected by the work of *speculation* itself and coincides with *humanism.* As *Feuerbach* represented *materialism* in the *theoretical* domain, French and English *socialism* and *communism* in the *practical* field represent *materialism* which now *coincides* with *humanism.*

'Speaking *exactly* and in the *prosaic* sense,' there are *two trends* in *French materialism*; one traces its origin to *Descartes,* the other to *Locke.* The latter is *mainly* a *French* development and leads direct to *socialism.* The former, *mechanical* materialism, merges with what is properly French *natural science.* The two trends cross in the course of development. We have no need here to go deep into French materialism, which comes direct from *Descartes,* and more than into the French *Newton* school or the development of French natural science in general.

We shall therefore just note the following:

Descartes in his *physics* endowed *matter* with self-creative power and conceived *mechanical* motion as the act of its life. He completely separated his *physics* from his *metaphysics. Within* his physics *matter* is the only *substance,* the only basis of being and of knowledge.

Mechanical French materialism followed *Descartes' physics* in opposition to his metaphysics. His followers were by profession *anti-metaphysicists,* i.e., *physicists.*

Voltaire observed that the indifference of Frenchmen to the disputes between Jesuits and Jansenists in the eighteenth century was due less to philosophy than to *Law's* financial speculation. And, in fact, the downfall of seventeenth-century metaphysics can be explained by the materialistic theory of the eighteenth century only as far as that theoretical movement itself is explained by the practical nature of French life at the time. That life was turned to the immediate present, worldly enjoyment and worldly interests, the *earthly* world. Its anti-theological, anti-metaphysical, and materialistic practice demanded corresponding anti-theological, anti-metaphysical and materialistic theories. Metaphysics had *in practice* lost all credit. Here we have only to indicate briefly the *theoretical* process.

In the seventeenth century metaphysics (cf. Descartes, Leibnitz, and others) still had an element of *positive,* profane content. It made discoveries in mathematics, physics and other exact sciences which seemed to come within its pale. This appearance was done away with as early as the beginning of the eighteenth century. The positive sciences broke off from it and determined their own separate fields. The whole wealth of metaphysics was reduced to beings of thought and heavenly things, although this was the very time when real beings and earthly things began to be the centre of all interest. Metaphysics had gone stale. In the very year in which Malebranche and Arnauld, the last great French metaphysicians of the seventeenth century, died, *Helvetius* and *Condillac* were born.

The man who deprived seventeenth-century metaphysics of all *credit* in the domain of *theory* was *Pierre Bayle*. His weapon was *scepticism*, which he forged out of metaphysics' own magic formulae. He at first proceeded from Cartesian metaphysics. As *Feuerbach* was driven by the fight against speculative theology to the fight against *speculative philosophy* precisely because he recognized in speculation the last prop of theology, because he had to force theology to turn back from pretended science to *coarse*, repulsive *faith*, so Bayle too was driven by religious doubt to doubt about metaphysics which was the support of that faith. He therefore critically investigated metaphysics from its very origin. He became its historian in order to write the history of its death. He mainly refuted *Spinoza* and *Leibnitz*.

Pierre Bayle did not only prepare the reception of materialism and the philosophy of common sense in France by shattering metaphysics with his scepticism. He heralded *atheistic society*, which was soon to come to existence, by *proving* that a society consisting only of atheists is *possible*, that an atheist *can* be a respectable man and that it is not by atheism but by superstition and idolatry that man debases himself.

To quote the expression of a French writer, *Pierre Bayle* was '*the last metaphysician in the seventeenth-century sense of the word and the first philosopher in the sense of the eighteenth century.*'

Besides the negative refutation of seventeenth-century theology and metaphysics, a *positive*, *anti-metaphysical* system was required. A book was needed which would systematize and theoretically justify the practice of life of the time. *Locke's* treatise on the origin of human reason came from across the Channel as if in answer to a call. It was welcomed enthusiastically like a long-awaited guest.

To the question: Was *Locke* perchance a follower of *Spinoƶa?* 'Profane' history may answer:

Materialism is the son of *Great Britain by birth*. Even Britain's scholastic *Duns Scotus* wondered: '*Can matter think?*'

In order to bring about that miracle he had recourse to God's omnipotence, i.e., he forced *theology* itself to preach *materialism*. In addition he was a *nominalist*. Nominalism is a main component of *English* materialism and is in general the *first expression* of materialism.

The real founder of *English materialism* and all *modern experimental* science was *Bacon*. For him natural science was true science and *physics* based on perception was the most excellent part of natural science. *Anaxagoras* with his *homoeomeria* and *Democritus* with his atoms are often the authorities he refers to. According to his teaching the *senses* are infallible and are the *source* of all knowledge. Science is *experimental* and consists in applying a *rational method* to the data provided by the senses. Induction, analysis, comparison, observation and experiment are the principal requisites of rational method. The first and most important of the inherent qualities of *matter* is *motion*, not only *mechanical* and *mathematical* movement, but still more *impulse, vital life-spirit, tension*, or, to use Jacob Bohme's expression, the *throes [Qual]* of matter. The primary forms of matter are the living, individualizing *forces of being* inherent in it and producing the distinctions between the species.

In *Bacon*, its first creator, materialism contained latent and still in a naïve way the germs of all-round development. Matter smiled at man with poetical sensuous brightness. The aphoristic doctrine itself, on the other hand, was full of the inconsistencies of theology.

In its further development materialism became *one-sided*. *Hobbes* was the one who *systematiƶed Bacon's* materialism. Sensuousness lost its bloom and became the abstract sensuousness of the *geometrician*. *Physical* motion was sacrificed to the *mechanical* or *mathematical, geometry* was proclaimed the principal science. Materialism became *hostile* to *humanity*. In order to overcome the *anti-human incorporeal* spirit in its own field, materialism itself was obliged to mortify its flesh and become an *ascetic*. It appeared as a *being of reason*, but it also developed the implacable logic of reason.

Hobbes systematised Bacon, but did not give a more precise proof of his basic principle that our knowledge and our ideas have their source in the world of the senses.

Locke proved the principle of Bacon and Hobbes in his essay on the origin of human reason.

The difference between *French* and *English* materialism follows from the difference between the two nations. The French imparted to English materialism wit, flesh and blood, and eloquence. They gave it the temperament and grace that it lacked. They *civilized* it.

In *Helvetius*, who also based himself on Locke, materialism became really French. Helvetius conceived it immediately in its application to social life (Helvetius, *De l'homme, de ses facultés intellectuelles et de son éducation*). Sensuous qualities and self-love, enjoyment and correctly understood personal interests are the bases of moral. The natural equality of human intelligence, the unity of progress of reason and progress of industry, the natural goodness of man and the omnipotence of education are the main points in his system.

In *Lamettrie's* works we find a combination of Descartes' system and English materialism. He makes use of Descartes' physics in detail. His '*Man Machine*' is a treatise after the model of Descartes' beast-machine. The physical part of Holbach's *Système de la nature, ou des lois du monde physique et du monde moral* is also a result of the combination of French and English materialism, while the moral part is based substantially on the moral of Helvetius. *Robinet* (*De la Nature*), the French materialist who had the most connection with metaphysics and was therefore praised by Hegel, refers explicitly to *Leibnitz*.

As *Cartesian* materialism merges into *natural science proper*, the other branch of French materialism leads direct to *socialism* and *communism*.

There is no need of any great penetration to see from the teaching of materialism on the original goodness and equal intellectual endowment of men, the omnipotence of experience, habit and education, and the influence of environment on man, the great significance of industry, the justification of enjoyment, etc., how necessarily materialism is connected with communism and socialism. If man draws all his knowledge, sensation, etc., from the world of the senses and the experience gained in it, the empirical world must be arranged so that in it man experiences and gets used to what is really human and that he becomes aware of himself as man. If correctly understood interest is the principle of all moral, man's private interest must be made to coincide with the interest of humanity. If man is unfree in the materialist sense, i.e., is free not through the negative power to avoid this or that, but through the positive power to assert his true individuality, crime must not be punished in the individual, but the anti-social source of crime must be destroyed, and each man must be given social scope for the vital manifestation of his being. If man is shaped by his surroundings, his surroundings must be made human. If man is social by nature, he will develop his true nature only in society, and the power of his nature must be measured not by the power of separate individuals but by the power of society.

This and similar propositions are to be found almost literally even in the oldest French materialists. This is not the place to assess them. *Fable of the Bees, or Private Vices Made Public Benefits*, by *Mandeville*, one of the early English followers of Locke, is typical of the social tendencies of materialism. He proves that in *modern* society vice is *indispensable* and *useful*. This was by no means an apology of modern society.

Fourier proceeds immediately from the teaching of the French materialists. The *Babouvists* were coarse, uncivilized materialists, but mature communism too comes *directly* from *French materialism*. The latter returned to its mother-country, *England*, in the form *Helvetius* gave it. *Bentham* based his system of *correctly understood interest* on Helvetius' moral, and *Owen* proceeded from *Bentham's* system to found English communism. Exiled to England, the Frenchman *Cabet* came under the influence of communist ideas there and on his return to France became the most popular, although the most superficial, representative of communism. Like Owen, the more scientific French communists, Dezamy, Gay and others, developed the teaching of *materialism* as the teaching of *real humanism* and the *logical* basis of *communism*.

H.F., pp. 168–177

[Marx's philosophy is rooted in that of the most influential of the early 19th century German philosophers, G. W. F. Hegel.

Hegel was an 'idealist'. In other words, he believed in the existence of something prior to man and matter. His thought can best be understood by way of the Christian analogy. Christians believe that God is prior to man and the world. Man is merely the material incarnation of God. But man has lapsed and fallen into imperfection. Awareness of this situation and of the path to redemption came through Jesus. The Christian strives to reintegrate himself in God, to be 'at one' with God.

Hegel's philosophy runs along parallel lines. Man is destined to be at one with 'Absolute Spirit'. This condition implies a sense of total identity with, and of mastery over, the objects which surround man (including the society in which he lives). Meanwhile Hegel's man is alienated from 'Absolute Spirit' just as Christian man is alienated from God. History is the process of becoming integrated. It is a process of increasing self-awareness, reflected in social change.

Marx objected, as we shall see later, to Hegel's idealism, his belief that mind and spirit are prior to man and matter. Nevertheless Marx's own method, like Hegel's, is dialectical – this is the core of his Hegelian inheritance. What is meant by 'dialectic'?

According to Hegel an existent (say, man) has potentialities embodied in its notion. (Thus the notion is prior to man.) The gulf between actual reality and potential reality is the starting point of the dialectical process. If we call the existent 'A', then its identity contains the contradiction of 'A' and 'non-A'. Thus 'A' is self-contradictory; it begets its own 'negation'. The negation is in turn self-contradictory and is negated. 'A' constantly surpasses itself in a process of continuous movement. For Marx, who imparted to dialectical movement a materialist basis, the process is inherent in the nature of things, and does not stem from the difference between the actual and the ideal which is prior to the actual, as Hegel argued.

The dialectic is not only an epistemological principle, a principle of knowing about knowing, but also an ontological one, a principle of knowing about being. Dialectic is both a method of knowing and a movement in the object known.

Marx, perhaps, transformed the structure of Hegel's dialectic by admitting the relative autonomy of ideas and superstructures. This may imply – the issue is disputed – that for Marx the primary economic contradiction is determinant only in the last instance and only in fusion with secondary, superstructure, factors. In this case, while Hegel's dialectic is based on a single, decisive contradiction, Marx's dialectic would seem to embrace] a plurality of contradictions within society.

My dialectic method is not only different from the Hegelian, but is its direct opposite. To Hegel, the life-process of the human brain, i.e., the process of thinking, which, under the name of 'the Idea', he even transforms into an independent subject, is the demiurgos of the real world, and the real world is only the external, phenomenal form of 'the Idea'. With me, on the contrary, the ideal is nothing else than the material world reflected by the human mind, and translated into forms of thought.

> Afterword to the
> Second German Edition of *Capital*   C.I., p. 19

. . . If one assumes religion and politics to be the basis of material living conditions, then it is only natural that everything should amount in the last instance to an investigation of human essence, i.e. of man's consciousness of himself. . . .

> G.I., p. 158

Hegel's conception of history assumes an *Abstract* or *Absolute Spirit* which develops in such a way that mankind is a mere

mass bearing it with a varying degree of consciousness or uncon-
sciousness. Within *empiric*, exoteric history he therefore has a
speculative, esoteric history develop. The history of mankind
becomes the history of the *abstract* spirit of mankind, a *spirit
beyond all man*!

Parallel with this doctrine of Hegel's there developed in
France that of the *Doctrinarians* proclaiming the *sovereignty of
reason* in opposition to the *sovereignty of the people* in order to
exclude the masses and rule *alone*. This was quite consistent. If
the activity of *real* mankind is nothing but the activity of a *mass*
of human individuals then *abstract generality, Reason*, the Spirit
must contrariwise have an abstract expression restricted to a
few individuals. It then depends on the situation and imaginative
power of each individual whether he will pass for a representative
of that 'spirit'.

In *Hegel* the *Absolute Spirit* of history already treats the *mass*
as material and finds its true expression only in *philosophy*.
But with Hegel, *the* philosopher is only the organ through
which the creator of history, the Absolute Spirit, arrives at
self-consciousness *by retrospection* after the movement has
ended. The participation of the philosopher in history is reduced
to this retrospective consciousness, for real movement is
accomplished by the Absolute Spirit *unconsciously*, so that the
philosopher appears *post festum*.

Hegel is doubly inconsistent; first because, while declaring
that philosophy constitutes the Absolute Spirit's existence he
refuses to recognize the *real philosophic individual* as the *Absolute*
Spirit; secondly, because according to him the Absolute Spirit
makes history only in *appearance*. For as the Absolute Spirit
becomes *conscious* of itself as the creative World Spirit only in
the philosopher and *post festum*, its making of history exists
only in the consciousness, in the opinion and conception of the
philosopher, i.e., only in the speculative imagination.

H.F., pp. 115–16

[In the passage which follows, Marx uses a sustained metaphor
to ridicule Hegelian idealism from his own materialist standpoint. Marx's materialism owed much to the works of Ludwig

Feuerbach, particularly to his *Critique of Hegelian Philosophy* (1839) and *The Essence of Christianity* (1841).

For Feuerbach, philosophy must begin with life, with sense perception. It is the human community which provides the community of meaning which makes truth and knowledge possible. Marx agreed, but gave to the concept of the human community a more historical social and economic basis. Marx's philosophy is a philosophy of history.]

If apples, pears, almonds and strawberries are really nothing but 'Substance', 'Fruit', the question arises: Why does 'Fruit' manifest itself to me sometimes as an apple, sometimes as a pear, sometimes as an almond? Why this *appearance of a diversity* which so strikingly contradicts my speculative conception of *'Unity'*; 'Substance'; 'Fruit'?

This, answers the speculative philosopher, is because fruit is not dead, undifferentiated, motionless, but living, self-differentiating, moving. The diversity of profane fruits is significant not only to *my* sensuous understanding, but also to 'Fruit' itself and to speculative reasoning. The different profane fruits are different manifestations of the life of the *one* 'Fruit'; they are crystallizations of 'Fruit' itself. In the apple 'Fruit' gives itself an apple-like existence, in the pear a pear-like existence. We must therefore no longer say as from the standpoint of Substance: a pear is 'Fruit,' an apple is 'Fruit,' an almond is 'Fruit,' but 'Fruit' presents itself as a pear, 'Fruit' presents itself as an apple, 'Fruit' presents itself as an almond; and the differences which distinguish apples, pears and almonds from one another are the self-differentiations of 'Fruit' making the particular fruits subordinate members of the life-process of 'Fruit.' Thus 'Fruit' is no longer a contentless, undifferentiated unity; it is oneness as *allness*, as *'totalness'* of fruits, which constitute an *'organic ramified series.'* In every member of that series 'Fruit' gives itself a more developed, more explicit existence, until it is finally the *'summary'* of all fruits and at the same time living *unity* which contains all those fruits dissolved in itself just as much as it produces them from within itself, as, for instance, all the limbs of the body are constantly dissolved in blood and constantly produced out of the blood.

We see that if the Christian religion knows only *one* Incarnation of God, speculative philosophy has as many incarnations as there are things, just as it has here in every fruit an incarnation of the 'Substance,' of the Absolute 'Fruit.' The main interest for the speculative philosopher is therefore to produce the *existence* of the real profane fruits and to say in some mysterious way that there are apples, pears, almonds and raisins. But the apples, pears, almonds and raisins that we get in the speculative world are nothing but *semblances* of apples, *semblances* of pears, *semblances* of almonds and *semblances* of raisins; they are moments in the life of 'Fruit,' that abstract *being of reason*, and therefore themselves abstract *beings of reason*. Hence what you enjoy in speculation is to find all the real fruits there, but as fruits which have a higher mystic significance, which are grown out of the ether of your brain and not out of the material earth, which are incarnations of 'Fruit,' *the Absolute Subject*. . . .
It goes without saying that the speculative philosopher accomplishes this constant creation only by representing universally known qualities of the apple, the pear, etc., which exist in reality, as definitions *discovered* by him; by giving the *names* of the real things to what abstract reason alone can create, to abstract formulae of reason; finally, by declaring his *own* activity, by which *he passes* from the idea of an apple to the idea of a pear, to be the *self-activity* of the Absolute Subject, 'Fruit.'

In the speculative way of speaking, this operation is called comprehending the *substance* as the *subject*, as an *inner process*, as an *Absolute Person* and that comprehension constitutes the essential character of *Hegel's* method.

H.F., pp. 79–82

In his *consciousness of species* man confirms his real *social life* and simply repeats his real existence in thought, just as conversely the being of the species confirms itself in species-consciousness and is for *itself* in its generality as a thinking being.

Man, much as he may therefore be a *particular* individual (and it is precisely his particularity which makes him an individual, and a real *individual* social being), is just as much the *totality* – the ideal totality – the subjective existence of thought and experienced society present for itself; just as he exists also in the real world as the awareness and the real enjoyment of social existence, and as a totality of human life-activity.

Thinking and being are thus no doubt *distinct*, but at the same time they are in *unity* with each other.

E.P.M., p. 105

The *sense* caught up in crude practical need has only a *restricted* sense. For the starving man, it is not the human form of food that exists, but only its abstract being as food; it could just as well be there in its crudest form, and it would be impossible to say wherein this feeding-activity differs from that of *animals*. The care-burdened man in need has no sense for the finest play; the dealer in minerals sees only the mercantile value but not the beauty and the unique nature of the mineral: he has no minera-logical sense. Thus, the objectification of the human essence both in its theoretical and practical aspects is required to make man's *sense human*, as well as to create the *human sense* corresponding to the entire wealth of human and natural substance.

E.P.M., p. 109

Sense-perception (see Feuerbach) must be the basis of all science. Only when it proceeds from sense-perception in the twofold form both of *sensuous* consciousness and of *sensuous* need – that is, only when science proceeds from nature – is it *true* science. All history is the preparation for '*man*' to become the object of *sensuous* consciousness, and for the needs of 'man as man' to become [natural, sensuous] needs. History itself is a *real* part of *natural history* – of nature's coming to be man. Natural science will in time subsume under itself the science of man, just as the science of man will subsume under itself natural science: there will be *one* science.

E.P.M., p. 111

Or perhaps Critical Criticism believes that it has got even to a *beginning* of the knowledge of historical reality while it still excludes *from* the historical movement the theoretical and practical relations of man to nature, natural science and industry? Or does it think that it actually knows any period without having knowledge, for example, of the industry of that period, the immediate mode of production of life itself? Of course, spiritualistic, *theological* Critical Criticism only knows (at least it imagines it knows) the main political, literary and theological acts of history. Just as it separates thinking from the senses, the soul from the body and itself from the world, it also separates history from natural science and industry and sees the origin of history not in *coarse material* production on the earth but in vaporous clouds in the heavens.   H.F., p. 201

The fact is, therefore, that definite individuals who are productively active in a definite way enter into these definite social and political relations. Empirical observation must in each separate instance bring out empirically, and without any mystification and speculation, the connection of the social and political structure with production. The social structure and the State are continually evolving out of the life-process of definite individuals, but of individuals, not as they may appear in their own or other people's imagination, but as they really are; i.e. as they are effective, produce materially, and are active under definite material limits, presuppositions and conditions independent of their will.   G.I., p. 13

[Marx quarrelled with his German contemporaries, the Young Hegelians and 'True Socialists' like Moses Hess and Bruno Bauer. They, like he, had rebelled against the existing state of Prussian society and government, which Hegel had towards the end of his life held up as the ultimate, ideal state. But they, unlike Marx, remained idealists for whom progress was critical or philosophic progress rather than material or social progress. Bauer wanted to expel all forms of religious dogma from the

human consciousness in order to eliminate all irrational elements
from the historic unfolding of reality. Marx wrote disparagingly
that the Young Hegelians taught the workers 'that they abolish
real capital by overcoming in *thinking* the category Capital ...]

The Old Hegelians had *comprehended* everything as soon as it
was reduced to an Hegelian logical category. The Young
Hegelians *criticized* everything by attributing to it religious
conceptions or by pronouncing it a theological matter. The
Young Hegelians are in agreement with the Old Hegelians in
their belief in the rule of religion, of concepts, of an abstract
general principle in the existing world. Only, the one party
attacks this dominion as usurpation, while the other extols it as
legitimate.

Since the Young Hegelians consider conceptions, thoughts,
ideas, in fact all the products of consciousness, to which they
attribute an independent existence, as the real chains of men
(just as the Old Hegelians declared them the true bonds of
human society) it is evident that the Young Hegelians have to
fight only against these illusions of the consciousness. Since,
according to their fantasy, the relationships of men, all their
doings, their chains and their limitations are products of their
consciousness, the Young Hegelians logically put to men the
moral postulate of exchanging their present consciousness for
human, critical or egoistic consciousness, and thus of removing
their limitations. This demand to change consciousness amounts
to a demand to interpret reality in another way, i.e. to accept
it by means of another interpretation. The Young-Hegelian
ideologists, in spite of their allegedly 'world-shattering' statements, are the staunchest conservatives. The most recent of
them have found the correct expression for their activity when
they declare they are only fighting against 'phrases'. They
forget, however, that to these phrases they themselves are only
opposing other phrases, and that they are in no way combating
the real existing world when they are merely combating the
phrases of this world. The only results which this philosophic
criticism could achieve were a few (and at that thoroughly one-
sided) elucidations of Christianity from the point of view of

religious history; all the rest of their assertions are only further embellishments of their claim to have furnished, in these unimportant elucidations, discoveries of universal importance.

It has not occurred to any one of these philosophers to inquire into the connection of German philosophy with German reality, the relation of their criticism to their own material surroundings. The premises from which we begin are not arbitrary ones, not dogmas, but real premises from which abstraction can only be made in the imagination. They are the real individuals, their activity and the material conditions under which they live, both those which they find already existing and those produced by their activity. These premises can thus be verified in a purely empirical way.

Men can be distinguished from animals by consciousness, by religion or anything else you like. They themselves begin to distinguish themselves from animals as soon as they begin to *produce* their means of subsistence, a step which is conditioned by their physical organization. By producing their means of subsistence men are indirectly producing their actual material life.

The way in which men produce their means of subsistence depends first of all on the nature of the actual means they find in existence and have to reproduce. This mode of production must not be considered simply as being the reproduction of the physical existence of the individuals. Rather it is a definite form of activity of these individuals, a definite form of expressing their life, a definite *mode of life* on their part. As individuals express their life, so they are. What they are, therefore, coincides with their production, both with *what* they produce and with *how* they produce. The nature of individuals thus depends on the material conditions determining their production.

G.I., pp. 5–7

B. Dialectical Materialism

[Influenced by the Hegelian dialectic, by the vision of man as something in the process of becoming, and influenced also by English, French and German (Feuerbach) materialism, as well as by the socialist ideas of Owen, Saint-Simon, Fourier and others, Marx was able to elaborate his mature philosophy, which we call dialectical materialism. Of course he did not derive inspiration from books alone; actual historic events, particularly the French Revolution and the subsequent victory of the European counter-revolution in 1815, also shaped his outlook.

Marx evolved what he regarded as a science of society and historical development. This belief in the existence of objective, determinable social laws was shared by the positivists, with whom Marx had much in common (although the positivism of Comte, unlike that of Saint-Simon, was conservative in tendency). Marx shared with the positivists the general optimism of the Enlightenment.]

What is to be avoided above all is the re-establishing of 'Society' as an abstraction *vis-à-vis* the individual. The individual is *the social being*. His life, even if it may not appear in the direct form of a *communal* life carried out together with others – is therefore an expression and confirmation of *social life*. Man's individual and species life are not *different*, however much – and this is inevitable – the mode of existence of the individual is a more *particular*, or more *general* mode of the life of the species, or the life of the species is a more *particular* or more *general* individual life.

E.P.M., p. 10

[But Marx remained more of a Hegelian than did Feuerbach. (Indeed it has been argued that Marx was not strictly a materialist at all.) The major contribution of Hegelian idealism was its insight into the essentially *active* relationship between man and the world, thought and matter. Unlike Feuerbach, Marx did not regard sensations as merely the experienced effects of things; they were the effects of the interaction between *active* man and his surroundings. Experience was a social as well as a biological dimension. Man has a history and a future; the world in which he lives and his consciousness of it are partly shaped by his purposes and his actions.]

The chief defect of all materialism up to now (including Feuerbach's) is, that the object, reality, what we apprehend through our senses, is understood only in the form of the *object* or *contemplation*; but not as *sensuous human activity*, as *practice*; not subjectively. Hence in opposition to materialism the *active* side was developed abstractly by idealism – which of course does not know real sensuous activity as such. Feuerbach wants sensuous objects, really distinguished from the objects of thought: but he does not understand human activity itself as *objective* activity. . . .

G.I., p. 197

The standpoint of the old type of materialism is civil society, the standpoint of the new materialism is human society or social humanity.

G.I., p. 199

The highest point to which contemplative materialism can attain, i.e. that materialism which does not comprehend our sensuous nature as practical activity, is the contemplation of separate individuals and of civil society.

G.I., p. 199

Feuerbach starts out from the fact of religious self-estrangement, of the duplication of the world into a religious and a secular one. His works consists in resolving the religious world into its secular basis. But that the secular basis raises itself above itself and establishes for itself an independent realm in the clouds can be explained only through the cleavage and self-contradictions within this secular basis. The latter must therefore in itself be both understood in its contradiction and revolutionized in practice. Therefore, after, e.g. the earthly family is discovered to be the secret of the heavenly family, one must proceed to destroy the former both in theory and in practice.

G.I., p. 198

All social life is essentially *practical*. All the mysteries which urge theory into mysticism find their rational solution in human practice and in the comprehension of this practice.

G.I., p. 199

The question whether objective truth is an attribute of human thought – is not a theoretical but a *practical* question. Man must prove the truth, i.e. the reality and power, the 'this-sidedness' of his thinking in practice. The dispute over the reality or non-reality of thinking that is isolated from practice is a purely *scholastic* question.

G.I., p. 197

The philosophers have only *interpreted* the world differently, the point is, to *change* it.

G.I., p. 199

[Marx thus introduced into his theory of knowledge a pragmatic element, making praxis – the interplay of mind, environment and activity – the decisive criterion of perception and of the understanding of reality. According to Marx, ideas are to be explained as creatures of their time. Does this mean that he denied the existence of objective truth?

Marx and Engels regarded the laws of mathematics and the principles of natural science as objectively verifiable. But philosophy and ideology in the era of class society had only a subjective significance, as reflections of conflicting social aspirations. In the classless society of the future thought would emerge as pure reason. Having grasped this connection, the material basis of mental evolution, Marx believed himself to have attained a new level of objectivity.

His emphasis on practice has another, more elementary significance. Asked whether he can be sure that the food on his plate is real, and not simply a figment of his imagination, a Marxist materialist answers: eat it and see.

There are a few well-known passages in Marx's writings which seem to sum up his philosophy as a whole. These passages leave no doubt that Marx regarded the economic factor as determinant. But in later life both Marx and Engels were anxious to dispel too crude an interpretation. Marx wrote that acceleration and delay in history depended on 'accidents', including the accident of the character of the leading figures of the age. In September 1890, Engels wrote: '. . . the economic factor finally asserts itself as necessary.'

Our conception of history depends on our ability to expound the real process of production, starting out from the simple material production of life, and to comprehend the form of intercourse connected with this and created by this (i.e. civil society in its various stages), as the basis of all history; further, to show it in its action as State; and so, from this starting-point, to explain the whole mass of different theoretical products and forms of consciousness, religion, philosophy, ethics etc. etc., and trace their origins and growth, by which means, of course, the whole thing can be shown in its totality (and therefore, too, the reciprocal action of these various sides on one another). It has not, like the idealistic view of history, in every period to look for a category, but remains constantly on the real ground of history; it does not explain practice from the idea but explains the formation of ideas from material practice; and accordingly it comes to the conclusion that all forms and products of consciousness cannot be dissolved by mental criticism, by resolution into 'self-consciousness' or transformation into 'apparitions', 'spectres', 'fancies', etc., but only by the practical overthrow of the actual social relations which gave rise to this idealistic humbug; that not criticism but revolution is the driving force of history, also of religion, of philosophy and all other types of theory. It shows that history does not end by being resolved into 'self-consciousness' as 'spirit of the spirit', but that in it at each stage there is found a material result: a sum of productive forces, a historically created relation of individuals to nature and to one another, which is handed down to each generation from its predecessor; a mass of productive forces, different forms of capital, and conditions, which, indeed, is modified by the new generation on the one hand, but also on the other prescribes for it its conditions of life and gives it a definite development, a special character. It shows that circumstances make men just as much as men make circumstances.

This sum of productive forces, forms of capital and social forms of intercourse, which every individual and generation finds in existence as something given, is the real basis of what the philosophers have conceived as 'substance' and 'essence of man', and what they have deified and attacked: a real basis which is not in the least disturbed, in its effect and influence on the development of men, by the fact that these philosophers revolt against it as 'self-consciousness' and 'the unique'. These conditions of life, which different generations find in existence, decide also whether or not the periodically recurring revolutionary convulsion will be strong enough to overthrow the basis of all existing forms. And if these material elements of a complete revolution are not present (namely, on the one hand the existence of productive forces, on the other the formation of a revolutionary mass, which revolts not only against separate conditions of society up till then, but against the very 'production of life' till then, the 'total activity' on which it was based), then, as far as practical development is concerned, it is absolutely immaterial whether the 'idea' of this revolution has been expressed a hundred times already; as the history of communism proves.

In the whole conception of history up to the present this real basis of history has either been totally neglected or else considered as a minor matter quite irrelevant to the course of history. History must therefore always be written according to an extraneous standard; the real production of life seems to be beyond history, while the truly historical appears to be separated from ordinary life, something extra-superterrestrial. With this the relation of man to nature is excluded from history and hence the antithesis of nature and history is created. The exponents of this conception of history have consequently only been able to see in history the political actions of princes and States, religious and all sorts of theoretical struggles, and in particular in each historical epoch have had to share the *illusion of that epoch*. For instance, if an epoch imagines itself to be actuated by purely 'political' or 'religious' motives, although 'religion' and 'politics' are only forms of its true motives, the historian accepts this opinion. The 'idea', the 'conception' of these conditioned men about their real practice, is transformed into the sole determining, active force, which controls and determines their practice. . . .

G.I., pp. 28–30

What is society, whatever its form may be? The product of men's reciprocal action. Are men free to choose this or that form of society for themselves? By no means. Assume a particular state of development in the productive forces of man and you will get a particular form of commerce and consumption. Assume particular stages of development in production, commerce and consumption and you will have a corresponding social constitution, a corresponding organization of the family, of orders or of classes, in a word, a corresponding civil society. Assume a particular civil society and you will get particular political conditions which are only the official expression of civil society. M. Proudhon* will never understand this because he thinks he is doing something great by appealing from the state

* P.-J. Proudhon, French social philosopher, anarchist and proponent of co-operative mutualism. Marx attacked his ideas in *The Poverty of Philosophy*.

to society – that is to say, from the official résumé of society to official society.

It is superfluous to add that men are not free to choose their *productive forces* – which are the basis of all their history – for every productive force is an acquired force, the product of former activity. The productive forces are therefore the result of practical human energy; but this energy is itself conditioned by the circumstances in which men find themselves, by the productive forces already acquired, by the social form which exists before they do, which they do not create, which is the product of the preceding generation. Because of this simple fact that every succeeding generation finds itself in possession of the productive forces acquired by the previous generation, which serve it as the raw material for new production, a coherence arises in human history, a history of humanity takes shape which is all the more a history of humanity as the productive forces of man and therefore his social relations have been more developed. Hence it necessarily follows that the social history of men is never anything but the history of their individual development, whether they are conscious of it or not. Their material relations are the basis of all their relations. These material relations are only the necessary forms in which their material and individual activity is realized.

M. Proudhon mixes up ideas and things. Men never relinquish what they have won, but this does not mean that they never relinquish the social form in which they have acquired certain productive forces. On the contrary, in order that they may not be deprived of the result attained, and forfeit the fruits of civilization, they are obliged, from the moment when the form of their commerce no longer corresponds to the productive forces acquired, to change all their traditional social forms. I am using the word 'commerce' here in its widest sense, as we use *Verkehr* in German. For example: the privileges, the institution of guilds and corporations, the regulatory regime of the Middle Ages, were social relations that alone corresponded to the acquired productive forces and to the social condition which had previously existed and from which these institutions had arisen. Under the protection of the regime of corporations and regulations, capital was accumulated, overseas trade was developed, colonies were founded. But the fruits of this men would have forfeited if they had tried to retain the forms under whose shelter these fruits had ripened. Hence burst two thunder-claps – the Revolutions of 1640 and 1688. All the old economic forms, the social relations corresponding to them, the political conditions which were the official expression of the old civil society, were destroyed in England. Thus the economic forms in which men produce, consume, and exchange, are *transitory* and *historical*. With the acquisition of new productive faculties, men change their mode of production and with the mode of production all the economic relations which are merely the necessary relations of this particular mode of production.

Marx to P. V. Annenkov, Dec. 28, 1846, P.P., pp. 180–2

The Manifesto being our joint production, I consider myself bound to state that the fundamental proposition, which forms its nucleus, belongs to Marx. That proposition is: that in every historical epoch, the prevailing mode of economic production and exchange, and the social organisation necessarily following from it, form the basis upon which is built up, and from which alone can be explained, the political and intellectual history of that epoch; that consequently the whole history of mankind (since the dissolution of primitive tribal society, holding land in common ownership) has been a history of class struggles, contests between exploiting and exploited, ruling and oppressed classes; that the history of these class struggles forms a series of evolutions in which, nowadays, a stage has been reached where the exploited and oppressed class – the proletariat – cannot attain its emancipation from the sway of the exploiting and ruling class – the bourgeoisie – without, at the same time, and once and for all, emancipating society at large from all exploitation, oppression, class distinctions and class struggles.

C.M., p. 23 (preface by Engels to the English edition of 1888)

... The general result at which I arrived and which, once won, served as a guiding thread for my studies, can be briefly for-mulated as follows: In the social production of their life, men

enter into definite relations that are indispensable and independent of their will, relations of production which correspond
to a definite stage of development of their material productive
forces. The sum total of these relations of production constitutes the economic structure of society, the real foundation, on
which rises a legal and political superstructure and to which
correspond definite forms of social consciousness. The mode
of production of material life conditions the social, political
and intellectual life process in general. It is not the consciousness
of men that determines their being, but, on the contrary, their
social being that determines their consciousness. At a certain
stage of their development, the material productive forces of
society come in conflict with the existing relations of production,
or – what is but a legal expression for the same thing – with the
property relations within which they have been at work hitherto.
From forms of development of the productive forces these
relations turn into their fetters. Then begins an epoch of social
revolution. With the change of the economic foundation the
entire immense superstructure is more or less rapidly transformed. In considering such transformations a distinction should
always be made between the material transformation of the
economic conditions of production, which can be determined
with the precision of natural science, and the legal, political,
religious, aesthetic or philosophic – in short, ideological forms
in which men become conscious of this conflict and fight it out.
Just as our opinion of an individual is not based on what he
thinks of himself, so can we not judge of such a period of
transformation by its own consciousness; on the contrary, this
consciousness must be explained rather from the contradictions
of material life, from the existing conflict between the social
productive forces and the relations of production. No social
order ever perishes before all the productive forces for which
there is room in it have developed; and new, higher relations of
production never appear before the material conditions of their
existence have matured in the womb of the old society itself.
Therefore mankind always sets itself only such tasks as it can
solve; since, looking at the matter more closely, it will always be
found that the task itself arises only when the material conditions
for its solution already exist or are at least in the process of
formation. In broad outlines Asiatic, ancient, feudal, and

modern bourgeois modes of production can be designated as progressive epochs in the economic formation of society. The bourgeois relations of production are the last antagonistic form of the social process of production – antagonistic not in the sense of individual antagonism, but of one arising from the social conditions of life of the individuals; at the same time the productive forces developing in the womb of bourgeois society create the material conditions for the solution of that antagonism. This social formation brings, therefore, the prehistory of human society to a close.

Preface to *A Contribution to the*
Critique of Political Economy, S.W.1, pp. 362–4

['Prehistory' is Marx's term for the epoch of class society – Asiatic, ancient, feudal, bourgeois. It suggests that 'history' itself only begins with classless, communist society – a conception which lays Marx open to the charge of teleology (of believing that history exists *in order that* truth may be brought to self-consciousness) which he himself levelled at the Hegelians in the passage which follows.

Some commentators have characterised Marx as a messianic or religious thinker. It would be more accurate to say that he was a perfectionist who mobilised material reality and empirical observation of it to the service of his own humanist ideal. Unlike truly religious thinkers, he acknowledged no reality] outside man and nature.

... *History* does *nothing*, it 'possesses *no* immense wealth,' it 'wages *no* battles.' It is *man*, real living man, that does all that, that possesses and fights; 'history' is not a person apart, using man as a means for *its own* particular aims; history is *nothing but* the activity of man pursuing his aims. ...

H.F., p. 125

PART TWO

The Human Predicament

A. The Alienation of Man

[Marx was inclined to reject any notion of an inherent, eternal human nature, as distinct from man's actual, and constantly changing, behaviour. Thus he attacks Feuerbach.]

Feuerbach resolves the essence of religion into the essence of *man*. But the essence of man is no abstraction inherent in each separate individual. In its reality it is the *ensemble* (aggregate) of social relations.

Feuerbach, who does not enter more deeply into the criticism of this real essence, is therefore forced:

1. To abstract from the process of history and to establish the religious temperament as something independent, and to postulate an abstract – *isolated* – human individual.

2. The essence of man can therefore be understood only as 'genus', the inward, dumb generality which *naturally* unites the many individuals.

G.I., pp. 198–9

The *natural sciences* have developed an enormous activity and have accumulated a constantly growing mass of material. Philosophy, however, has remained just as alien to them as they remain to philosophy. Their momentary unity was only a *chimerical illusion*. The will was there, but the means were lacking. Even historiography pays regard to natural science only occasionally, as a factor of enlightenment and a utility arising from individual great discoveries. But natural science has invaded and transformed human life all the more *practically* through the medium of industry; and has prepared human emancipation, however directly and much it had to consummate dehumanisation. *Industry* is the *actual*, historical relation of nature, and therefore of natural science, to man. If, therefore, industry is conceived as the *exoteric* revelation of man's *essential powers*, we also gain an understanding of the *human* essence of nature or the *natural* essence of man. In consequence, natural science will lose its abstractly material – or rather, its idealistic – tendency, and will become the basis of *human* science, as it has already become the basis of actual human life, albeit in an estranged form. *One* basis for life and another basis for *science* is *a priori* a lie. The nature which comes to be in human history – the genesis of human society – is man's *real* nature; hence nature as it comes to be through industry, even though in an *estranged* form, is true *anthropological* nature.

E.P.M., pp. 110–11

[Here the emphasis has changed. There is, after all, a 'true, anthropological nature'. Indeed, a vision of social man as he ultimately must become emerges as the genesis of dialectical materialism. Marx shared Hegel's refusal to accept an imperfect world. In an early work (1843), Marx wrote: 'The criticism of religion ends with the doctrine that *man is the supreme being for man*. It ends, therefore, with the *categorical imperative to overthrow all those conditions* in which man is an abased, enslaved, abandoned, contemptible being . . .'

Nothing could be more clear. The term by which both Hegel and Marx described man's unfulfilled condition was 'alienation' (*Entfremdung*). Marx followed Hegel in describing man's progress towards fulfilment as the overcoming of a situation in which man's own products and other men appeared in the guise of alien, hostile objects. But Marx, as usual, criticised Hegel's idealist formulation of the problem.]

There is a double error in Hegel.

The first emerges most clearly in the *Phenomenology*, the Hegelian philosophy's place of origin. When, for instance, wealth, state-power, etc., are understood by Hegel as entities estranged from the *human* being, this only happens in their form as thoughts . . . They are thought-entities, and therefore merely an estrangement of *pure*, i.e., abstract, philosophical thinking. The whole process therefore ends with Absolute Knowledge. It is precisely abstract thought from which these objects are estranged and which they confront with their arrogation of reality. The *philosopher* sets himself (that is, one who is himself an abstract form of estranged man) as the *measuring-rod* of the estranged world. The whole *history of the alienation-process* and the whole *process of the retraction* of the alienation is therefore nothing but the *history of the production* of abstract (i.e., absolute) thought – of logical, speculative thought.

E.P.M., pp. 148–9

[Under the influence of Feuerbach, Marx originally regarded alienation as man's self-alienation, an anthropological condition. This was the basis of Feuerbach's explanation of religion. Marx's acquaintance Moses Hess ascribed to money the same significance as Feuerbach ascribed to religion – a point which impressed Marx.]

Objectification is the practice of alienation. Just as man, so long as he is engrossed in religion, can only objectify his essence by an *alien* and fantastic being; so under the sway of egoistic need, he can only affirm and produce objects in practice by subordinating his products and his own activity to the domination of an alien entity, and by attributing to them the significance of an alien entity, namely money.

'Bruno Bauer, "The Capacity of the present-day Jews and Christians to become free"'   E.W., p. 39

Money, then, appears as this *overturning* power both against the individual and against the bonds of society, etc., which claim to be *essences* in themselves. It transforms fidelity into infidelity, love into hate, hate into love, virtue into vice, vice into virtue, servant into master, master into servant, idiocy into intelligence and intelligence into idiocy.

E.P.M., p. 141

[By 1844 the theory of self-alienation was giving way to a more social perspective. Marx came to regard the division of labour and alienated labour in class society as the root of the condition. Alienated man is divided against his fellow men and therefore against himself. This concept takes on an increasingly social and economic complexion, while the anthropological interpretation recedes.]

. . . Labour produces not only commodities: it produces itself and the worker as a *commodity* – and does so in the proportion in which it produces commodities generally.

This fact expresses merely that the object which labour produces – labour's product – confronts it as *something alien*, as a *power independent* of the producer. The product of labour is labour which has been congealed in an object, which has become material: it is the *objectification* of labour. Labour's realisation is its objectification. In the conditions dealt with by political economy this realisation of labour appears as *loss of reality* for the workers; objectification as *loss of the object* and *object-bondage*; appropriation as *estrangement*, as *alienation*.

E.P.M., p. 69

When we ask, then, what is the essential relationship of labour we are asking about the relationship of the *worker* to production.

Till now we have been considering the estrangement, the alienation of the worker only in one of its aspects, i.e., the worker's *relationship to the products of his labour*. But the estrangement is manifested not only in the result but in the *act of production* – within the *productive activity* itself. How would the worker come to face the product of his activity as a stranger, were it not that in the very act of production he was estranging himself from himself? The product is after all but the summary of the activity, of production. If then the product of labour is alienation, production itself must be active alienation, the alienation of activity, the activity of alienation. In the estrangement of the object of labour is merely summarised the estrangement, the alienation, in the activity of labour itself.

What, then, constitutes the alienation of labour?

First, the fact that labour is *external* to the worker, i.e., it does not belong to his essential being; that in his work, therefore, he does not affirm himself but denies himself, does not feel content but unhappy, does not develop freely his physical and mental energy but mortifies his body and ruins his mind. The worker therefore only feels himself outside his work, and in his work feels outside himself. He is at home when he is not working, and when he is working he is not at home. His labour is therefore not voluntary, but coerced; it is *forced labour*. It is therefore not the satisfaction of a need; it is merely *a means* to satisfy needs external to it. Its alien character emerges clearly in the fact that as soon as no physical or other compulsion exists, labour is shunned like the plague. External labour, labour in which man alienates himself, is a labour of self-sacrifice, of mortification. Lastly, the external character of labour for the worker appears in the fact that it is not his own, but someone else's, that it does not belong to him, that in it he belongs, not to himself, but to another. Just as in religion the spontaneous activity of the human imagination, of the human brain and the human heart, operates independently of the individual – that is, operates on him as an alien, divine or diabolical activity – in the same way the worker's activity is not his spontaneous activity. It belongs to another; it is the loss of his self.

E.P.M., pp. 72–73

We must bear in mind the above-stated proposition that man's relation to himself only becomes *objective* and *real* for him through his relation to the other man. Thus, if the product of his labour, his labour *objectified*, is for him an *alien*, hostile, powerful object independent of him, then his position towards it is such that someone else is master of this object, someone who is alien, hostile, powerful, and independent of him. If his own activity is to him an unfree activity, then he is treating it as activity performed in the service, under the dominion, the coercion and the yoke of another man.

Every self-estrangement of man from himself and from nature appears in the relation in which he places himself and nature to men other than and differentiated from himself. For this reason religious self-estrangement necessarily appears in the relationship of the layman to the priest, or again to a mediator, etc., since we are here dealing with the intellectual world. In the real practical world self-estrangement can only become manifest through the real practical relationship to other men. The medium through which estrangement takes place is itself *practical*. Thus through estranged labour man not only engenders his relationship to the object and to the act of production as to powers that are alien and hostile to him; he also engenders the relationship in which other men stand to his production and to his product, and the relationship in which he stands to these other men. Just as he begets his own production as the loss of his reality, as his punishment; just as he begets his own product as a loss, as a product not belonging to him; so he begets the dominion of the one who does not produce over production and over the product. Just as he estranges from himself his own activity, so he confers to the stranger activity which is not his own.

E.P.M., pp. 79–80

This *material*, immediately *sensuous* private property is the material sensuous expression of *estranged human* life. Its movement – production and consumption – is the *sensuous* revelation of the movement of all production hitherto – i.e., the realisation or the reality of man. Religion, family, state, law, morality, science, art, etc., are only *particular* modes of production, and fall under its general law. The positive transcendence of *private property* as the appropriation of *human* life is, therefore, the positive transcendence of all estrangement – that is to say, the return of man from religion, family, state, etc., to his *human*, i.e., *social* mode of existence. Religious estrangement as such occurs only in the realm of *consciousness*, of man's inner life, but economic estrangement is that of *real life*; its transcendence therefore embraces both aspects. . . .

E.P.M., p. 103

The propertied class and the class of the proletariat present the same human self-alienation. But the former class finds in this self-alienation its confirmation and its good, *its own power*: it has in it a *semblance* of human existence. The class of the proletariat feels annihilated in its self-alienation; it sees in it its own powerlessness and the reality of an inhuman existence. In the words of Hegel, the class of the proletariat is in abasement *indignation* at that abasement, an indignation to which it is necessarily driven by the contradiction between its human *nature* and its condition of life, which is the outright, decisive and comprehensive negation of that nature.

Within this antithesis the private owner is therefore the *conservative* side, the proletarian, the *destructive* side. From the former arises the action of preserving the antithesis, from the latter, that of annihilating it.

H.F., p. 51

But the exercise of labour power, labour, is the worker's own life-activity, the manifestation of his own life. And this *life-activity* he sells to another person in order to secure the necessary *means of subsistence*. Thus his life-activity is for him only a means to enable him to exist. He works in order to live. He does not even reckon labour as part of his life, it is rather a sacrifice of his life. It is a commodity which he has made over to another. Hence, also, the product of his activity is not the object of his activity. What he produces for himself is not the silk that he weaves, not the gold that he draws from the mine, not the palace that he builds. What he produces for himself is *wages*, and silk, gold, palace resolve themselves for him into a definite quantity of the means of subsistence, perhaps into a cotton jacket, some copper coins and a lodging in a cellar. And the worker, who for twelve hours weaves, spins, drills, turns, builds, shovels, breaks stones, carries loads, etc. – does he consider his twelve hours' weaving, spinning, drilling, turning, building, shovelling, stone breaking as a manifestation of his life, as life? On the contrary, life begins for him where this activity ceases, at table, in the public house, in bed. The twelve hours' labour, on the other hand, has no meaning for him as weaving, spinning, drilling, etc., but as *earnings*, which bring him to the table, to the public house, into bed. . . .

Wage Labour and Capital   S.W.I., pp. 82–83

[In the later writings the word alienation disappears. Class society is described in more functional and sociological terms, and less in general anthropological terms. But two aspects of the alienation concept remain: the 'false consciousness' of the property-owning classes, and the 'fetishism of commodities' (man-made objects becoming alien and hostile to their creators). This is known as the reification principle, and is discussed in *Capital* as a general feature of human relations in capitalist society.

The division within the workshop mirrors that in society. The problem of the assembly-line worker is familiar to modern industrial psychologists. When in the 1840's Proudhon had suggested that a solution would be found if the productive process were no longer fragmented, Marx had mocked him for wanting to go back to the middle ages (P.P., p. 144). He still regarded the root of alienation as being the mode of production, the structure of ownership, the division of society into classes. But *Capital* revealed a greater awareness of the role of machinery and of the division of labour within the workshop in the process of alienation. Machinery, Marx wrote, 'converts the labourer into a crippled monstrosity'. The third volume of *Capital* even proposes that the 'realm of freedom' and the 'development of human personality for its own sake' can begin only after working hours. This suggests that even under communism men will not attain true freedom so long as they are compelled to work.]

A commodity is therefore a mysterious thing, simply because in it the social character of men's labour appears to them as an objective character stamped upon the product of that labour; because the relation of the producers to the sum total of their own labour is presented to them as a social relation, existing not between themselves, but between the products of their labour. This is the reason why the products of labour become commodities, social things whose qualities are at the same time perceptible and imperceptible by the senses. . . . There it is a definite social relation between men, that assumes, in their eyes, the fantastic form of a relation between things. In order, therefore, to find an analogy, we must have recourse to the mist-enveloped regions of the religious world. In that world the productions of the human brain appear as independent beings endowed with life, and entering into relation both with one another and the human race. So it is in the world of commodities with the products of men's hands. This I call the Fetishism which attaches itself to the products of labour, so soon as they are produced as commodities, and which is therefore inseparable from the production of commodities.

This Fetishism of commodities has its origin, as the foregoing analysis has already shown, in the peculiar social character of the labour that produces them.

C.I., p. 72

The knowledge, the judgment, and the will, which, though in ever so small a degree, are practised by the independent peasant or handicraftsman, in the same way as the savage makes the whole art of war consist in the exercise of his personal cunning – these faculties are now required only for the workshop as a whole. Intelligence in production expands in one direction, because it vanishes in many others. What is lost by the detail labourers, is concentrated in the capital that employs them. It is a result of the division of labour in manufactures, that the labourer is brought face to face with the intellectual potencies of the material process of production, as the property of another, and as a ruling power. This separation begins in simple co-operation, where the capitalist represents to the single workman, the oneness and the will of the associated labour. It is developed in manufacture which cuts down the labourer into a detail labourer. It is completed in modern industry, which makes science a productive force distinct from labour and presses it into the service of capital.

In manufacture, in order to make the collective labourer, and through him capital, rich in social productive power, each labourer must be made poor in individual productive powers. . . .

C.I., p. 361

Some crippling of body and mind is inseparable even from division of labour in society as a whole. Since, however, manufacture carries this social separation of branches of labour much further, and also, by its peculiar division, attacks the individual at the very roots of his life, it is the first to afford the materials for, and to give a start to, industrial pathology.

'To subdivide a man is to execute him, if he deserves the sentence, to assassinate him if he does not . . . The subdivision of labour is the assassination of a people.'   C.I., p. 363

[It is therefore open to doubt whether in his last years Marx maintained the social optimism and confidence of this passage] from *The German Ideology* (1846).

Thus things have now come to such a pass, that the individuals must appropriate the existing totality of productive forces, not only to achieve self-activity, but, also, merely to safeguard their very existence. This appropriation is first determined by the object to be appropriated, the productive forces, which have been developed to a totality and which only exist within a universal intercourse. From this aspect alone, therefore, this appropriation must have a universal character corresponding to the productive powers and the intercourse. The appropriation of these powers is itself nothing more than the development of the individual capacities corresponding to the material instruments of production. The appropriation of a totality of instruments of production is, for this very reason, the development of a totality of capacities in the individuals themselves.

G.I., p. 66

B. Class and Class Struggle

[According to Marx, man's alienation takes the social form of class struggle.

No concept is more fundamental to Marxism. Yet Marx himself never fully defined a social class. His notes on the subject, included in the third volume of *Capital* (edited by Engels) break off in mid-stream. But Marx's general conceptions about social classes and their behaviour are fairly clear.]

The first question to be answered is this: What constitutes a class? – and the reply to this follows naturally from the reply to another question, namely: What makes wage-labourers, capitalists and landlords constitute the three great social classes?

At first glance – the identity of revenues and sources of revenue. There are three great social groups whose members, the individuals forming them, live on wages, profit and ground-rent respectively, on the realization of their labour-power, their capital, and their landed property.

However, from this standpoint, physicians and officials, e.g., would also constitute two classes, for they belong to two distinct social groups, the members of each of these groups receiving their revenue from one and the same source. The same would also be true of the infinite fragmentation of interest and rank into which the division of social labour splits labourers as well as capitalists and landlords – the latter, e.g., into owners of vineyards, farm owners, owners of forests, mine owners and owners of fisheries.

[Here the manuscript breaks off.]   C.III., pp. 862–3

The owners merely of labour-power, owners of capital, and landowners, whose respective sources of income are wages, profit and ground rent, in other words, wage-labourers, capitalists and landowners, constitute then three big classes of modern society based upon the capitalist mode of production.

In England, modern society is indisputably most highly and classically developed in economic structure. Nevertheless, even here the stratification of classes does not appear in its pure form. Middle and intermediate strata even here obliterate lines of demarcation everywhere (although incomparably less in rural districts than in the cities). However, this is immaterial for our analysis. We have seen that the continual tendency and law of development of the capitalist mode of production is more and more to divorce the means of production from labour, and more and more to concentrate the scattered means of production into large groups, thereby transforming labour into wage-labour and the means of production into capital. And to this tendency, on the other hand, corresponds the independent separation of landed property from capital and labour, or the transformation of all landed property into the form of landed property corresponding to the capitalist mode of production.

C.III.

. . . What is the basis of a partial, merely political revolution? Simply this: a *section of civil society* emancipates itself and attains universal domination; a determinate class undertakes, from its *particular situation*, a general emancipation of society. This class emancipates society as a whole, but only on condition that the whole of society is in the same situation as this class; for example, that it possesses or can easily acquire money or culture.

No class in civil society can play this part unless it can arouse, in itself and in the masses, a moment of enthusiasm in which it associates and mingles with society at large, identifies itself with it, and is felt and recognized as the *general representative* of this society. Its aims and interests must genuinely be the aims and interests of society itself, of which it becomes in reality the social head and heart. It is only in the name of general interests that a particular class can claim general supremacy. In order to attain this liberating position, and the political direction of all spheres of society, revolutionary energy and consciousness of its own power do not suffice. For a *popular revolution* and the *emancipation of a particular class* of civil society to coincide, for *one* class to represent the whole of society, another class must concentrate in itself all the evils of society, a particular class must embody and represent a general obstacle and limitation. A particular social sphere must be regarded as the *notorious crime* of the whole society, so that emancipation from this sphere appears as a general emancipation. For *one* class to be the liberating class *par excellence*, it is necessary that another class should be openly the oppressing class. The negative significance of the French nobility and clergy produced the positive significance of the bourgeoisie, the class which stood next to them and opposed them.

Contribution to the Critique
of Hegel's Philosophy of Right   E.W., pp. 55-56

... For each new class which puts itself in the place of one ruling before it, is compelled, merely in order to carry through its aim, to represent its interest as the common interest of all the members of society, put in an ideal form; it will give its ideas the form of universality, and represent them as the only rational, universally valid ones. The class making a revolution appears from the very start, merely because it is opposed to a *class*, not as a class but as the representative of the whole of society; it appears as the whole mass of society confronting the one ruling class. It can do this because, to start with, its interest really is more connected with the common interest of all other non-ruling classes, because under the pressure of conditions its interest has not yet been able to develop as the particular interest of a particular class. Its victory, therefore, benefits also many individuals of the other classes which are not winning a dominant position, but only in so far as it now puts these individuals in a position to raise themselves into the ruling class. When the French bourgeoisie overthrew the power of the aristocracy, it thereby made it possible for many proletarians to raise themselves above the proletariat, but only in so far as they became bourgeois. Every new class, therefore, achieves its hegemony only on a broader basis than that of the class ruling previously, in return for which the opposition of the non-ruling class against the new ruling class later develops all the more sharply and profoundly. Both these things determine the fact that the struggle to be waged against this new ruling class, in its turn, aims at a more decided and radical negation of the previous conditions of society than could all previous classes which sought to rule.

This whole semblance, that the rule of a certain class is only the rule of certain ideas, comes to a natural end, of course, as soon as society ceases at last to be organised in the form of class-rule, that is to say as soon as it is no longer necessary to represent a particular interest as general or 'the general interest' as ruling.

G.I., pp. 40–41

Further, it follows that every class which is struggling for mastery, even when its domination, as is the case with the proletariat, postulates the abolition of the old form of society in its entirety and of mastery itself, must first conquer for itself political power in order to represent its interest in turn as the general interest, a step to which in the first moment it is forced. . . .

G.I., p. 23

An oppressed class is the vital condition for every society founded on the antagonism of classes. The emancipation of the oppressed class thus implies necessarily the creation of a new society. For the oppressed class to be able to emancipate itself it is necessary that the productive powers already acquired and the existing social relations should no longer be capable of existing side by side. Of all the instruments of production, the greatest productive power is the revolutionary class itself. The organisation of revolutionary elements as a class supposes the existence of all the productive forces which could be engendered in the bosom of the old society.

P.P., pp. 173–4

Meanwhile the antagonism between the proletariat and the bourgeoisie is a struggle of class against class, a struggle which carried to its highest expression is a total revolution. Indeed, is it at all surprising that a society founded on the opposition of classes should culminate in brutal *contradiction*, the shock of body against body, as its final *dénouement?*

Do not say that social movement excludes political movement. There is never a political movement which is not at the same time social.

It is only in an order of things in which there are no more classes and class antagonisms that *social evolutions* will cease to be *political revolutions*. Till then, on the eve of every general reshuffling of society, the last word of social science will always be:

'*Le combat ou la mort; la lutte sanguinaire ou le néant. C'est ainsi que la question est invinciblement posée.*' (Georges Sand)

P.P., pp. 174–5

[Pre-capitalist, feudal society is marked by the dominance of the landed aristocracy. Thus the rise of the bourgeoisie, and the bourgeois revolution, takes place at the expense of the landowners. Here we notice that the rivalry of aristocrats and bourgeois is a predominantly *political* one; the two classes do not exist in *direct* economic antagonism to one another, because they possess quite different means of production, the one rural and the other urban. The later struggle between capitalists and proletarians, on the other hand, is both political and economic. It is to the capitalist that the worker sells his labour-power.

Marx uses the term 'bourgeois' very widely. Not only capitalists but also professional men and the middle classes in general normally come under this category. Yet if we define – as Marx himself seems to – a social class by its relationship to the means of production, we notice at once that a professional man may derive his income from wages, more like a proletarian than like a capitalist. But Marx includes him in the bourgeoisie. This can only be because Marx implicitly acknowledged at least two other criteria for defining class: status and function. First, as regards status. The education, family background, level of income, standard of living, etc., of a civil servant link him in diverse ways to the capitalist class, to the bourgeoisie. After all, no one argues that a capitalist's wife is any the less bourgeois for not *owning* her husband's factory. Secondly, function: the civil servant serves the bourgeois state and its values. Unfortunately, Marx never managed to incorporate such diverse criteria into a systematic and explicit theory of class.

Marx points out that members of a single class may be in mutual rivalry. This need not necessarily be economic rivalry (as with competition between capitalists) but also, as Marx's *The Class Struggles in France, 1848–50*, indicates, political rivalry as well. These divisions are explained by distinguishing between the needs of the financial, industrial and commercial bourgeoisie.

In the Middle Ages the citizens in each town were compelled to unite against the landed nobility to save their skins. The extension of trade, the establishment of communications, led the separate towns to get to know other towns, which had asserted the same interests in the struggle with the same antagonist. Out of the many local corporations of burghers there arose only gradually the burgher *class*. The conditions of life of the individual burghers became, on account of their antagonism to the existing relationships and of the mode of labour determined by these, conditions which were common to them all and independent of each individual. The burghers had created the conditions in so far as they had torn themselves free from feudal ties, and were created by them in so far as they were determined by their antagonism to the feudal system which they found in existence. When the individual towns began to enter into associations, these common conditions developed into class conditions. The same conditions, the same antagonism, the same interests necessarily called forth on the whole similar customs everywhere. The bourgeoisie itself, with its conditions, develops only gradually, splits according to the division of labour into various fractions and finally absorbs all earlier possessing classes (while it develops the majority of the earlier non-possessing, and a part of the earlier possessing, class into a new class, the proletariat) in the measure to which all earlier property is transformed into industrial or commercial capital. The separate individuals form a class only in so far as they have to carry on a common battle against another class; otherwise they are on hostile terms with each other as competitors. On the other hand, the class in its turn achieves an independent existence over against the individuals, so that the latter find their conditions of existence predestined, and hence have their position in life and their personal development assigned to them by their class, become subsumed under it. This is the same phenomenon as the subjection of the separate individuals to the division of labour and can only be removed by the abolition of private property and of labour itself. We have already indicated several times how this subsuming of individuals under the class brings with it their subjection to all kinds of ideas, etc.

G.I., pp. 48–49

The bourgeoisie begins with a proletariat which is itself a relic of the proletariat of feudal times. In the course of its historical development, the bourgeoisie necessarily develops its antagonistic character, which at first is more or less disguised, existing only in a latent state. As the bourgeoisie develops, there develops in its bosom a new proletariat, a modern proletariat; there develops a struggle between the proletarian class and the bourgeois class, a struggle which, before being felt, perceived, appreciated, understood, avowed and proclaimed aloud by both sides, expresses itself, to start with, merely in partial and momentary conflicts, in subversive acts. On the other hand, if all the members of the modern bourgeoisie have the same interests inasmuch as they form a class as against another class, they have opposite, antagonistic interests, inasmuch as they stand face to face with one another. This opposition of interests results from the economic conditions of their bourgeois life. From day to day it thus becomes clearer that the production relations in which the bourgeoisie moves have not a simple, uniform character, but a dual character; that in the self-same relations in which wealth is produced, poverty is produced also; that in the self-same relations in which there is a development of the productive forces, there is also a force producing repression; that these relations produce *bourgeois wealth*, i.e., the wealth of the bourgeois class, only by continually annihilating the wealth of the individual members of this class and by producing an ever-growing proletariat.

P.P., pp. 122–3

In the bourgeoisie we have two phases to distinguish: that in which it constituted itself as a class under the regime of feudalism and absolute monarchy, and that in which, already constituted as a class, it overthrew feudalism and monarchy to make society into a bourgeois society. The first of these phases was the longer and necessitated the greater efforts. This too began by partial combination against the feudal lords.

P.P., p. 173

The modern bourgeois society that has sprouted from the ruins of feudal society has not done away with class antagonisms. It has but established new classes, new conditions of oppression, new forms of struggle in place of the old ones.

Our epoch, the epoch of the bourgeoisie, possesses, however, this distinctive feature: it has simplified the class antagonisms. Society as a whole is more and more splitting up into two great hostile camps, into two great classes directly facing each other: Bourgeoisie and Proletariat.

From the serfs of the Middle Ages sprang the chartered burghers of the earliest towns. From these burgesses the first elements of the bourgeoisie were developed.

The discovery of America, the rounding of the Cape, opened up fresh ground for the rising bourgeoisie. The East-Indian and Chinese markets, the colonisation of America, trade with the colonies, the increase in the means of exchange and in commodities generally, gave to commerce, to navigation, to industry, an impulse never before known, and thereby, to the revolutionary element in the tottering feudal society, a rapid development.

The feudal system of industry, under which industrial production was monopolised by closed guilds, now no longer sufficed for the growing wants of the new markets. The manufacturing system took its place. The guild-masters were pushed on one side by the manufacturing middle class; division of labour between the different corporate guilds vanished in the face of division of labour in each single workshop.

Meantime the markets kept ever growing, the demand ever rising. Even manufacture no longer sufficed. Thereupon, steam and machinery revolutionised industrial production. The place of manufacture was taken by the giant, Modern Industry, the place of the industrial middle class, by industrial millionaires, the leaders of whole industrial armies, the modern bourgeois.

Modern industry has established the world market, for which the discovery of America paved the way. This market has given an immense development to commerce, to navigation, to communication by land. This development has, in its turn, reacted on the extension of industry; and in proportion as industry, commerce, navigation, railways extended, in the same proportion the bourgeoisie developed, increased its capital, and pushed into the background every class handed down from the Middle Ages.

We see, therefore, how the modern bourgeoisie is itself the product of a long course of development, of a series of revolutions in the modes of production and of exchange.

Each step in the development of the bourgeoisie was accompanied by a corresponding political advance of that class. An oppressed class under the sway of the feudal nobility, an armed and self-governing association in the mediaeval commune; here independent urban republic (as in Italy and Germany), there taxable 'third estate'* of the monarchy (as in France), afterwards, in the period of manufacture proper, serving either the semi-feudal or the absolute monarchy as a counterpoise against the

* Marx does not mean that the 'third estate' was identical with the bourgeoisie in 18th century France. An estate is not a class; it is a political and juridical category. The third estate included everyone who was neither a priest nor a nobleman. Nevertheless, bourgeois revolutionaries were able to rally the masses to the slogan 'Vive le tiers Etat!' after 1789. Ed.

nobility, and, in fact, corner-stone of the great monarchies in general, the bourgeoisie has at last, since the establishment of Modern Industry and of the world market, conquered for itself, in the modern representative State, exclusive political sway. The executive of the modern State is but a committee for managing the common affairs of the whole bourgeoisie.

The bourgeoisie, historically, has played a most revolutionary part.

The bourgeoisie, wherever it has got the upper hand, has put an end to all feudal, patriarchal, idyllic relations. It has pitilessly torn asunder the motley feudal ties that bound man to his 'natural superiors', and has left remaining no other nexus between man and man than naked self-interest, than callous 'cash payment'. It has drowned the most heavenly ecstasies of religious fervour, of chivalrous enthusiasm, of philistine sentimentalism, in the icy water of egotistical calculation. It has resolved personal worth into exchange value, and in place of the numberless indefeasible chartered freedoms, has set up that single, unconscionable freedom – Free Trade. In one word, for exploitation, veiled by religious and political illusions, it has substituted naked, shameless, direct, brutal exploitation.

The bourgeoisie has stripped of its halo every occupation hitherto honoured and looked up to with reverent awe. It has converted the physician, the lawyer, the priest, the poet, the man of science, into its paid wage-labourers.

The bourgeoisie has torn away from the family its sentimental veil, and has reduced the family relation to a mere money relation. C.M., pp. 46–50

The bourgeoisie cannot exist without constantly revolutionising the instruments of production, and thereby the relations of production, and with them the whole relations of society. Conservation of the old modes of production in unaltered form, was, on the contrary, the first condition of existence for all earlier industrial classes. Constant revolutionising of production, uninterrupted disturbance of all social conditions, everlasting uncertainty and agitation distinguish the bourgeois epoch from all earlier ones. All fixed, fast-frozen relations, with their train of ancient and venerable prejudices and opinions, are swept away, all new-formed ones become antiquated before they can ossify. All that is solid melts into air, all that is holy is profaned, and man is at last compelled to face with sober senses, his real conditions of life, and his relations with his kind.

The need of a constantly expanding market for its products chases the bourgeoisie over the whole surface of the globe. It must nestle everywhere, settle everywhere, establish connexions everywhere.

The bourgeoisie has through its exploitation of the world market given a cosmopolitan character to production and consumption in every country. To the great chagrin of Reactionists, it has drawn from under the feet of industry the national ground on which it stood. All old-established national industries have been destroyed or are daily being destroyed. . . .

C.M., pp. 51–52

The bourgeoisie, by the rapid improvement of all instruments of production, by the immensely facilitated means of communication, draws all, even the most barbarian, nations into civilisation. The cheap prices of its commodities are the heavy artillery with which it batters down all Chinese walls, with which it forces the barbarians' intensely obstinate hatred of foreigners to capitulate. It compels all nations, on pain of extinction, to adopt the bourgeois mode of production; it compels them to introduce what it calls civilisation into their midst, i.e., to become bourgeois themselves. In one word, it creates a world after its own image.

The bourgeoisie has subjected the country to the rule of the towns. It has created enormous cities, has greatly increased the urban population as compared with the rural, and has thus rescued a considerable part of the population from the idiocy of rural life. Just as it has made the country dependent on the towns, so it has made barbarian and semi-barbarian countries dependent on the civilised ones, nations of peasants on nations of bourgeois, the East on the West.   C.M., p. 53

[Do the peasants constitute a social class? When discussing France, Marx refers to the 'peasant class', but when discussing Germany he distinguishes between peasant proprietors and the rural proletariat (landless labourers). Lenin was later to base his strategy of revolution in Russia on this distinction.

In an oft-quoted passage (see below) Marx suggests that the peasants of France constitute a class in so far as they live 'under economic conditions' that separate 'their mode of life, their interests and their culture from other classes'. But they were not fully a class on account of their failure to develop the necessary political and class consciousness.

Marx expected the peasant farmer to be extinguished by large-scale capitalist farming and forced down into a vast agricultural proletariat.

The small-holding peasants form a vast mass, the members of which live in similar conditions but without entering into manifold relations with one another. Their mode of production isolates them from one another instead of bringing them into mutual intercourse. The isolation is increased by France's bad means of communication and by the poverty of the peasants. Their field of production, the small holding, admits of no division of labour in its cultivation, no application of science and, therefore, no diversity of development, no variety of talent, no wealth of social relationships. Each individual peasant family is almost self-sufficient; it itself directly produces the major part of its consumption and thus acquires its means of life more through exchange with nature than in intercourse with society. A small holding, a peasant and his family; alongside them another small holding, another peasant and another family. A few score of these make up a village, and a few score of villages make up a Department. In this way, the great mass of the French nation is formed by simple addition of homologous magnitudes, much as potatoes in a sack form a sack of potatoes. In so far as millions of families live under economic conditions of existence that separate their mode of life, their interests and their culture from those of the other classes, and put them in hostile opposition to the latter, they form a class. In so far as there is merely a local interconnection among these small-holding peasants, and the identity of their interests begets no community, no national bond and no political organisation among them, they do not form a class. They are consequently incapable of enforcing their class interests in their own name, whether through a parliament or through a convention. They cannot represent themselves, they must be represented. Their representative must at the same time appear as their master, as an authority over them, as an unlimited governmental power that protects them against the other classes and sends them rain and sunshine from above. The political influence of the small-holding peasants, therefore, finds its final expression in the executive power subordinating society to itself.

The 18th Brumaire of Louis Bonaparte   S.W.i., p. 334

The economic development of small-holding property has radically changed the relation of the peasants to the other classes of society. Under Napoleon, the fragmentation of the land in the countryside supplemented free competition and the beginning of big industry in the towns. The peasant class was the ubiquitous protest against the landed aristocracy which had just been overthrown. The roots that small-holding property struck in French soil deprived feudalism of all nutriment. Its landmarks formed the natural fortifications of the bourgeoisie against any surprise attack on the part of its old overlords. But in the course of the nineteenth century the feudal lords were replaced by urban usurers; the feudal obligation that went with the land was replaced by the mortgage; aristocratic landed property was replaced by bourgeois capital. The small holding of the peasant is now only the pretext that allows the capitalist to draw profits, interest and rent from the soil, while leaving it to the tiller of the soil himself to see how he can extract his wages. The mortgage debt burdening the soil of France imposes on the French peasantry payment of an amount of interest equal to the annual interest on the entire British national debt. Small-holding property, in this enslavement by capital to which its development inevitably pushes forward, has transformed the mass of the French nation into troglodytes. Sixteen million peasants (including women and children) dwell in hovels, a large number of which have but one opening, others only two and the most favoured only three. And windows are to a house what the five senses are to the head. The bourgeois order, which at the beginning of the century set the state to stand guard over the newly arisen small holding and manured it with laurels, has become a vampire that sucks out its blood and brains and throws them into the alchemistic cauldron of capital. The *Code Napoléon* is now nothing but a *codex* of distraints, forced sales and compulsory auctions. To the four million (including children, etc.) officially recognised paupers, vagabonds, criminals and prostitutes in France must be added five million who hover on the margin of existence and either have their haunts in the countryside itself or, with their rags and their children, continually desert the countryside for the towns and the towns for the countryside. The interests of the peasants, therefore, are no longer, as under Napoleon, in accord with, but in opposition to the interests of the bourgeoisie, to capital. Hence the peasants find their natural ally and leader in the *urban proletariat*, whose task is the overthrow of the bourgeois order.

The 18th Brumaire of Louis Bonaparte   S.W.I., pp. 337–8

[Marx's *original* interest in the proletariat was not based on empirical observation or the first-hand knowledge which inspired Engels' *Condition of the Working Class in England* (1844). Marx first wrote of the proletariat late in 1843, as a result of reading about conditions in France. At this stage he thought of the worker not so much as a wage-slave as the prototype of man in a state of alienation, the ultimate victim of an irrational society. The worker represented the most extreme degradation of man. Propertyless and without illusions, his aspirations were therefore the universal aspirations of mankind.

But after his arrival in Paris late in 1843 and his serious study of political economy, Marx began to locate the worker more concretely in the capitalist system. Also, unlike many other socialists, Marx now regarded the proletariat as a class destined *to emancipate itself* by force.]

Where is there, then, a *real* possibility of emancipation in Germany?

This is our reply. A class must be formed which has *radical chains*, a class in civil society which is not a class of civil society, a class which is the dissolution of all classes, a sphere of society which has a universal character because its sufferings are universal, and which does not claim a *particular redress* because the wrong which is done to it is not a *particular wrong* but *wrong in general*. There must be formed a sphere of society which claims no *traditional* status but only a human status, a sphere which is not opposed to particular consequences but is totally opposed to the assumptions of the German political system; a sphere, finally, which cannot emancipate itself without emancipating itself from all the other spheres of society, without, therefore, emancipating all these other spheres, which is, in short, a *total loss* of humanity and which can only redeem itself by a *total redemption of humanity*. This dissolution of society, as a particular class, is the *proletariat*.

Contribution to the Critique of
Hegel's Philosophy of Right   E.W., p. 58

Private property as private property, as wealth, is compelled to maintain *itself*, and thereby its opposite, the proletariat, in *existence*. That is the *positive* side of the contradiction, self-satisfied private property.

The proletariat, on the other hand, is compelled as proletariat to abolish itself and thereby its opposite, the condition for its existence, what makes it the proletariat, i.e., private property. That is the *negative* side of the contradiction, its restlessness within its very self, dissolved and self-dissolving private property.   H.F., p. 51

. . . The question is not what this or that proletarian, or even the whole of the proletariat at the moment *considers* as its aim. The question is *what the proletariat is*, and what, consequent on that *being*, it will be compelled to do. Its aim and historical action is irrevocably and obviously demonstrated in its own life situation as well as in the whole organisation of bourgeois society today. There is no need to dwell here upon the fact that a large part of the English and French proletariat is already *conscious* of its historical task and is constantly working to develop that consciousness into complete clarity.

H.F., p. 53

. . . And finally, while the bourgeoisie of each nation still retained separate national interests, big industry created a class, which in all nations has the same interest and with which nationality is already dead; a class which is really rid of all the old world and at the same time stands pitted against it. For the worker it makes not only the relation to the capitalist, but labour itself, unbearable.

It is evident that big industry does not reach the same level of development in all districts of a country. This does not, however, retard the class movement of the proletariat, because the proletarians created by big industry assume leadership of this movement and carry the whole mass along with them, and because the workers excluded from big industry are placed by it in a still worse situation than the workers in big industry themselves. The countries in which big industry is developed act in a similar manner upon the more or less non-industrial countries, in so far as the latter are swept by universal commerce into the universal competitive struggle. . . .

G.I., pp. 57–58

Economic conditions had first transformed the mass of the people of the country into workers. The combination of capital has created for this mass a common situation, common interests. This mass is thus already a class as against capital, but not yet for itself. In the struggle, of which we have noted only a few phases, this mass becomes united, and constitutes itself as a class for itself. The interests it defends become class interests. But the struggle of class against class is a political struggle.

P.P., p. 173

In the conditions of the proletariat, those of old society at large are already virtually swamped. The proletarian is without property; his relation to his wife and children has no longer anything in common with the bourgeois family relations; modern industrial labour, modern subjection to capital, the same in England as in France, in America as in Germany, has stripped him of every trace of national character. Law, morality, religion, are to him so many bourgeois prejudices, behind which lurk in ambush just as many bourgeois interests.

All the preceding classes that got the upper hand, sought to fortify their already acquired status by subjecting society at large to their conditions of appropriation. The proletarians cannot become masters of the productive forces of society, except by abolishing their own previous mode of appropriation, and thereby also every other previous mode of appropriation. They have nothing of their own to secure and to fortify; their mission is to destroy all previous securities for, and insurances of, individual property.

All previous historical movements were movements of minorities, or in the interest of minorities. The proletarian movement is the self-conscious, independent movement of the immense majority, in the interest of the immense majority. The proletariat, the lowest stratum of our present society, cannot stir, cannot raise itself up, without the whole superincumbent strata of official society being sprung into the air.

Though not in substance, yet in form, the struggle of the proletariat with the bourgeoisie is at first a national struggle. The proletariat of each country must, of course, first of all settle matters with its own bourgeoisie.

C.M., pp. 65–66

[For the misfits of society, the 'Bohemians', the rootless drifters, Marx had nothing but scorn. *Their* condition of alienation lacked revolutionary potential, and therefore did not interest him.]

. . . On the pretext of founding a benevolent society, the *lumpenproletariat* of Paris had been organised into secret sections, each section being led by Bonapartist agents, with a Bonapartist general at the head of the whole. Alongside decayed *roués* with dubious means of subsistence and of dubious origin, alongside ruined and adventurous offshoots of the bourgeoisie, were vagabonds, discharged soldiers, discharged jailbirds, escaped galley slaves, swindlers, mountebanks, *lazzaroni*, pick-pockets, tricksters, gamblers, *maquereaus*, brothel keepers, porters, *literati*, organ-grinders, rag-pickers, knife grinders, tinkers, beggars – in short, the whole indefinite, disintegrated mass, thrown hither and thither, which the French term *la bohème*; from this kindred element Bonaparte formed the core of the Society of December 10. A 'benevolent society' – in so far as, like Bonaparte, all its members felt the need of benefiting themselves at the expense of the labouring nation. This Bonaparte, who constitutes himself *chief of the lumpenproletariat*, who here alone rediscovers in mass form the interests which he personally pursues, who recognises in this scum, offal, refuse of all classes the only class upon which he can base himself unconditionally, is the real Bonaparte, the Bonaparte *sans phrase*. . . .

The 18th Brumaire of
Louis Bonaparte S.W.I., pp. 294–5

[The passage which follows raises an important problem. If ideological attitudes are conditioned by class, how is it that Marx and Engels, who were 'bourgeois', not only proclaimed the proletarian revolution but actively worked for it? Marx suggests here, and elsewhere, that it is not a question of compassion but of scientific comprehension of the historical process. But why do some members of the bourgeoisie objectively and rationally comprehend the historical process while the majority remain imprisoned by class prejudice? If it is a matter of intelligence and insight, then the thesis that ideological positions are determined by class has to be modified. Marx's explanation also leaves unsolved the problem of why recognition of what is *ultimately* inevitable should entail activity on its behalf. (Of course Marx and Engels had a moral and emotional commitment to the working class, but they preferred not to stress this lest it undermine the scientific character of their theory.)

This passage also indicates that Marx envisages the ultimate reduction of mankind under capitalism to two antagonistic classes: a small class of immensely wealthy monopolists, and a huge, revolutionary proletariat.]

Finally, in times when the class struggle nears the decisive hour, the process of dissolution going on within the ruling class, in fact within the whole range of old society, assumes such a violent, glaring character, that a small section of the ruling class cuts itself adrift, and joins the revolutionary class, the class that holds the future in its hands. Just as, therefore, at an earlier period, a section of the nobility went over to the bourgeoisie, so now a portion of the bourgeoisie goes over to the proletariat, and in particular, a portion of the bourgeois ideologists, who have raised themselves to the level of comprehending theoretically the historical movement as a whole.

Of all the classes that stand face to face with the bourgeoisie today, the proletariat alone is a really revolutionary class. The other classes decay and finally disappear in the face of modern industry; the proletariat is its special and essential product.

The lower middle class, the small manufacturer, the shopkeeper, the artisan, the peasant, all these fight against the bourgoisie, to save from extinction their existence as fractions of the middle class. They are therefore not revolutionary, but conservative. Nay more, they are reactionary, for they try to roll back the wheel of history. If by chance they are revolutionary, they are so only in view of their impending transfer into the proletariat, they thus defend not their present, but their future interests, they desert their own standpoint to place themselves at that of the proletariat.

The 'dangerous class', the social scum, that passively rotting mass thrown off by the lowest layers of old society, may, here and there, be swept into the movement by a proletarian revolution; its conditions of life, however, prepare it far more for the part of a bribed tool of reactionary intrigue.

C.M., pp. 63–65

Darwin, whom I have looked up again, amuses me when he says he is applying the 'Malthusian' theory *also* to plants and animals, as if with Mr. Malthus* the whole point were not that he does *not* apply the theory to plants and animals but only to human beings – and with geometrical progression – as opposed to plants and animals. It is remarkable how Darwin recognises among beasts and plants his English society with its division of labour, competition, opening up of new markets, 'inventions', and the Malthusian 'struggle for existence'. It is Hobbes's *bellum omnium contra omnes*, and one is reminded of Hegel's *Phenomenology*, where civil society is described as a 'spiritual animal kingdom', while in Darwin the animal kingdom figures as civil society . . .

Marx to Engels, June 18, 1862   S.C., pp. 156–7

* Thomas Malthus, who in 1798 published his 'Essay on the Principle of Population. . . .' and argued that population would always increase more rapidly than the means of subsistence. Thus distress and want among the lower orders was a law of nature, and palliatives were useless. Marx poured scorn on Malthus, not because he believed in the possibility of reforming capitalist society, but because he regarded the jungle-law of capitalism as only a transitory historical phase. Ed.

C. Consciousness

[The link between the human predicament (alienation, class struggle) and the revolutionary act is revolutionary consciousness. Following Feuerbach, Marx advances a materialist explanation of consciousness in general, at the same time insisting that consciousness is immanent in economic and social relations – in history.]

The production of ideas, of conceptions, of consciousness, is at first directly interwoven with the material activity and the material intercourse of men, the language of real life. Conceiving, thinking, the mental intercourse of men, appear at this stage as the direct efflux of their material behaviour. The same applies to mental production as expressed in the language of the politics, laws, morality, religion, metaphysics of a people. Men are the producers of their conceptions, ideas, etc. – real, active men, as they are conditioned by a definite development of their productive forces and of the intercourse corresponding to these, up to its furthest forms. Consciousness can never be anything else than conscious existence, and the existence of men is their actual life-process. If in all ideology men and their circumstances appear upside down as in a *camera obscura*, this phenomenon arises just as much from their historical life-processes as the inversion of objects on the retina does from their physical life-process.   G.I., pp. 13–14

In direct contrast to German philosophy which descends from heaven to earth, here we ascend from earth to heaven. That is to say, we do not set out from what men say, imagine, conceive, nor from men as narrated, thought of, imagined, conceived, in order to arrive at men in the flesh. We set out from real, active men, and on the basis of their real life-process we demonstrate the development of the ideological reflexes and echoes of this life-process. The phantoms formed in the human brain are also, necessarily, sublimates of their material life-process, which is empirically verifiable and bound to material premises. Morality, religion, metaphysics, all the rest of ideology and their corresponding forms of consciousness, thus no longer retain the semblance of independence. They have no history, no development; but men, developing their material production and their material intercourse, alter, along with this their real existence, their thinking and the products of their thinking. Life is not determined by consciousness, but consciousness by life. In the first method of approach the starting-point is consciousness taken as the living individual; in the second it is the real living individuals themselves, as they are in actual life, and consciousness is considered solely as *their* consciousness.

G.I., pp. 14–15

. . . Consciousness is therefore from the very beginning a social product, and remains so as long as men exist at all. Consciousness is at first, of course, merely consciousness concerning the immediate sensuous environment and consciousness of the limited connection with other persons and things outside the individual who is growing self-conscious. At the same time it is consciousness of nature, which first appears to men as a completely alien, all-powerful and unassailable force, with which men's relations are purely animal and by which they are overawed like beasts; it is thus a purely animal consciousness of nature (natural religion).

We see here immediately: this natural religion or animal behaviour towards nature is determined by the form of society and *vice versa*. Here, as everywhere, the identity of nature and man appears in such a way that the restricted relation of men to nature determines their restricted relation to one another, and their restricted relation to one another determines men's restricted relation to nature, just because nature is as yet hardly modified historically; and, on the other hand, man's consciousness of the necessity of associating with the individuals around him is the beginning of the consciousness that he is living in society at all. This beginning is as animal as social life itself at this stage. It is mere herd-consciousness, and at this point man is only distinguished from sheep by the fact that with him consciousness takes the place of instinct or that his instinct is a conscious one.

This sheep-like or tribal consciousness receives its further development and extension through increased productivity, the increase of needs, and, what is fundamental to both of these, the increase of population. With these there develops the division of labour, which was originally nothing but the division of labour in the sexual act, then that division of labour which develops spontaneously or 'naturally' by virtue of natural predisposition (e.g. physical strength), needs, accidents, etc., etc. Division of labour only becomes truly such from the moment when a division of material and mental labour appears. From this moment onwards consciousness *can* really flatter itself that it is something other than consciousness of existing practice, that it is *really* conceiving something without conceiving something *real*; from now on consciousness is in a position to emancipate itself from the world and to proceed to the formation of 'pure' theory, theology, philosophy, ethics, etc. But even if this theory, theology, philosophy, ethics, etc. comes into contradiction with the existing relations, this can only occur as a result of the fact that existing social relations have come into contradiction with existing forces of production; this, moreover, can also occur in a particular national sphere of relations through the appearance of the contradiction, not within the national orbit, but between this national consciousness and the practice of other nations, i.e. between the national and the general consciousness of a nation.

Moreover, it is quite immaterial what consciousness starts to do on its own: out of all such muck we get only the one inference that these three moments, the forces of production, the state of society, and consciousness, can and must come into contradiction with one another, because the division of labour implies the possibility, nay the fact that intellectual and material activity – enjoyment and labour, production and consumption – devolve on different individuals, and that the only possibility of their not coming into contradiction lies in the negation in its turn of the division of labour. It is self-evident, moreover, that 'spectres', 'bonds', 'the higher being', 'concept', 'scruple', are merely the idealistic, spiritual expression, the conception apparently of the isolated individual, the image of very empirical fetters and limitations, within which the mode of production of life, and the form of intercourse coupled with it, move.

G.I., pp. 19–21

[Feuerbach had described religion as the projection and hypostasis of an element of human experience into an object of worship. Religion reflected man's impotence in the world, his ignorance of its laws. 'The more empty life is, the fuller, the more concrete, is God.' Saint-Simon adopted a similar view.

Marx's theory of religion appears to oscillate between such a general materialist explanation and a more specifically social and economic one. Religion is at one time described as the 'opium of the people' and at another as an instrument whereby the ruling class sanctifies its privileges. It is in one place 'a protest against real suffering' and in another a creed which preaches 'the necessity of a ruling and an oppressed class'. Possibly these apparent contradictions could partly be resolved by distinguishing between creed and cult, God and Church. But Marx did not achieve any sustained analysis, and, as was often the case, penetrated the problem with more power than refinement.]

The basis of irreligious criticism is this: *man makes religion*; religion does not make man. Religion is indeed man's self-consciousness and self-awareness so long as he has not found himself or has lost himself again. But *man* is not an abstract being, squatting outside the world. Man is *the human world*, the state, society. This state, this society, produce religion which is an *inverted world consciousness*, because they are an *inverted world*. Religion is the general theory of this world, its encyclopedic compendium, its logic in popular form, its spiritual *point d'honneur*, its enthusiasm, its moral sanction, its solemn complement, its general basis of consolation and justification. It is the *fantastic realization* of the human being inasmuch as the *human being* possesses no true reality. The struggle against religion is, therefore, indirectly a struggle against *that world* whose spiritual *aroma* is religion.

Religious suffering is at the same time an *expression* of real suffering and a *protest* against real suffering. Religion is the sigh of the oppressed creature, the sentiment of a heartless world, and the soul of soulless conditions. It is the *opium* of the people.

Contribution to the Critique of
Hegel's Philosophy of Right.   E.W., pp. 43–44

The religious world is but the reflex of the real world. And for a society based upon the production of commodities, in which the producers in general enter into social relations with one another by treating their products as commodities and values, whereby they reduce their individual private labour to the standard of homogeneous human labour – for such a society, Christianity with its *cultus* of abstract man, more especially in its bourgeois developments, Protestantism, Deism, &c., is the most fitting form of religion. . . . The religious reflex of the real world can, in any case, only then finally vanish, when the practical relations of every-day life offer to man none but perfectly intelligible and reasonable relations with regard to his fellowmen and to Nature.   C.I., p. 79

The social principles of Christianity have now had eighteen hundred years to develop and need no further development by Prussian consistorial councillors.

The social principles of Christianity justified the slavery of Antiquity, glorified the serfdom of the Middle Ages and equally know, when necessary, how to defend the oppression of the proletariat, although they make a pitiful face over it.

The social principles of Christianity preach the necessity of a ruling and an oppressed class, and all they have for the latter is the pious wish the former will be charitable.

The social principles of Christianity transfer the consistorial councillors' adjustment of all infamies to heaven and thus justify the further existence of these infamies on earth.

The social principles of Christianity declare all vile acts of the oppressors against the oppressed to be either the just punishment of original sin and other sins or trials that the Lord in his infinite wisdom imposes on those redeemed.

The social principles of Christianity preach cowardice, self-contempt, abasement, submission, dejection, in a word all the qualities of the *canaille*; and the proletariat, not wishing to be treated as *canaille*, needs its courage, its self-feeling, its pride and its sense of independence more than its bread.

The social principles of Christianity are sneakish and the proletariat is revolutionary.

So much for the social principles of Christianity.

> The Communism of the Paper
> 'Rheinischer Beobachter'.   O.R., pp. 83–84

[Marx teaches that consciousness in class society is primarily class consciousness. The ideas of the ruling class are, consequently, the ruling ideas of the age. As a revolutionary class arises, revolutionary ideas challenge the ruling ideas.

Marx did not believe that class ideologies are in general consciously hypocritical. Instead, he postulated the notion of 'false consciousness' – the unconscious rationalisation, or deification, in universal terms of narrow self-interest. But when discussing particular bourgeois politicians of his own day, Marx easily imputed to them conscious dishonesty.

Marx and Engels regarded scientific and mathematical laws as existing independently of class consciousness. But it is not clear how far 'ideology', the class-conditioned sphere, is supposed to extend. Presumably the categories of thought and speech of which the diverging ideologies are composed have to be explained in general materialist terms rather than in specifically class terms. But Marx leaves the question open.]

Does it require deep intuition to comprehend that man's ideas, views and conceptions, in one word, man's consciousness, changes with every change in the conditions of his material existence, in his social relations and in his social life?

What else does the history of ideas prove, than that intellectual production changes its character in proportion as material production is changed? The ruling ideas of each age have ever been the ideas of its ruling class.

C.M., pp. 80–81

The ideas of the ruling class are in every epoch the ruling ideas: i.e. the class, which is the ruling material force of society, is at the same time its ruling intellectual force. The class which has the means of material production at its disposal, has control at the same time over the means of mental production, so that thereby, generally speaking, the ideas of those who lack the means of mental production are subject to it. The ruling ideas are nothing more than the ideal expression of the dominant material relationships, the dominant material relationships grasped as ideas; hence of the relationships which make the one class the ruling one, therefore the ideas of its dominance. The individuals composing the ruling class possess among other things consciousness, and therefore think. In so far, therefore, as they rule as a class and determine the extent and compass of an epoch, it is self-evident that they do this in their whole range, hence among other things rule also as thinkers, as producers of ideas, and regulate the production and distribution of the ideas of their age: thus their ideas are the ruling ideas of the epoch. For instance, in an age and in a country where royal power, aristocracy and bourgeoisie are contending for mastery and where, therefore, mastery is shared, the doctrine of the separation of powers proves to be the dominant idea and is expressed as an 'eternal law'. The division of labour, which we saw above as one of the chief forces of history up till now, manifests itself also in the ruling class as the division of mental and material labour, so that inside this class one part appears as the thinkers of the class (its active, conceptive ideologists, who make the perfecting of the illusion of the class about itself their chief source of livelihood), while the others' attitude to these ideas and illusions is more passive and receptive, because they are in reality the active members of this class and have less time to make up illusions and ideas about themselves. Within this class this cleavage can even develop into a certain opposition and hostility between the two parts, which, however, in the case of a practical collision, in which the class itself is endangered, automatically comes to nothing, in which case there also vanishes the semblance that the ruling ideas were not the ideas of the ruling class and had a power distinct from the power of this class. The existence of revolutionary ideas in a particular period presupposes the existence of a revolutionary class; about the premises for the latter sufficient has already been said above.

If now in considering the course of history we detach the ideas of the ruling class from the ruling class itself and attribute to them an independent existence, if we confine ourselves to saying that these or those ideas were dominant, without bothering ourselves about the conditions of production and the producers of these ideas, if we then ignore the individuals and world conditions which are the source of the ideas, we can say, for instance, that during the time that the aristocracy was dominant, the concepts honour, loyalty, etc., were dominant, during the dominance of the bourgeoisie the concepts freedom, equality, etc. The ruling class itself on the whole imagines this to be so. This conception of history, which is common to all historians, particularly since the eighteenth century, will necessarily come up against the phenomenon that increasingly abstract ideas hold sway, i.e. ideas which increasingly take on the form of universality. . . .

G.I., pp. 39–40

None of the supposed rights of man, therefore, go beyond the egoistic man, man as he is, as a member of civil society; that is, an individual separated from the community, withdrawn into himself, wholly preoccupied with his private interest and acting in accordance with his private caprice. Man is far from being considered, in the rights of man, as a species-being; on the contrary, species-life itself – society – appears as a system which is external to the individual and as a limitation of his original independence. The only bond between men is natural necessity, need and private interest, the preservation of their property and their egoistic persons.

'Bruno Bauer, "Die Judenfrage".'   E.W., p. 26

. . . Only one must not form the narrow-minded notion that the petty bourgeoisie, on principle, wishes to enforce an egoistic class interest. Rather, it believes that the *special* conditions of its emancipation are the *general* conditions within the frame of which alone modern society can be saved and the class struggle avoided. Just as little must one imagine that the democratic representatives are indeed all shopkeepers or enthusiastic champions of shop-keepers. According to their education and their individual position they may be as far apart as heaven from earth. What makes them representatives of the petty bourgeoisie is the fact that in their minds they do not get beyond the limits which the latter do not get beyond in life, that they are consequently driven, theoretically, to the same problems and solutions to which material interest and social position drive the latter practically. This is, in general, the relationship between the *political* and *literary representatives* of a class and the class they represent.

The 18th Brumaire of Louis Bonaparte   S.W.I., p. 275

[It is philosophy (i.e. scientific socialism) which, according to Marx, brings to the proletariat consciousness of its role. Marx believed that the proletariat required such an awareness in order to be revolutionary; suffering alone was not enough. On the other hand the revolutionary bourgeoisie had evidently triumphed in its time without any such self-awareness.]

Just as philosophy finds its *material* weapons in the proletariat, so the proletariat finds its *intellectual* weapons in philosophy. And once the lightning of thought has penetrated deeply into this virgin soil of the people, the *Germans* will emancipate them-selves and become *men*.

. . . In Germany *no* type of enslavement can be abolished unless *all* enslavement is destroyed. Germany, which likes to get to the bottom of things, can only make a revolution which upsets *the whole order* of things. The *emancipation of Germany* will be an *emancipation of man*. *Philosophy* is the *head* of this emancipation and the *proletariat* is its *heart*. Philosophy can only be realized by the abolition of the proletariat, and the proletariat can only be abolished by the realization of philosophy.

> Contribution to the Critique of
> Hegel's Philosophy of Right.   E.W., p. 59

Just as the *economists* are the scientific representatives of the bourgeois class, so the *Socialists* and the *Communists* are the theoreticians of the proletarian class. So long as the proletariat is not yet sufficiently developed to constitute itself as a class, and consequently so long as the struggle itself of the proletariat with the bourgeoisie has not yet assumed a political character, and the productive forces are not yet sufficiently developed in the bosom of the bourgeoisie itself to enable us to catch a glimpse of the material conditions necessary for the emancipation of the proletariat and for the formation of a new society, these theoreticians are merely utopians who, to meet the wants of the oppressed classes, improvise systems and go in search of a regenerating science. But in the measure that history moves forward, and with it the struggle of the proletariat assumes clearer outlines, they no longer need to seek science in their minds; they have only to take note of what is happening before their eyes and to become its mouthpiece. So long as they look for science and merely make systems, so long as they are at the beginning of the struggle, they see in poverty nothing but poverty, without seeing in it the revolutionary, subversive side, which will overthrow the old society. From this moment, science, which is a product of the historical movement, has associated itself consciously with it, has ceased to be doctrinaire and has become revolutionary.

> P.P., pp. 125–6

PART THREE

Capitalism

A. Economic Categories

[Marx's main achievement after 1850 was to work out in formidable economic detail the sociological principles he had advanced before 1848.

The first four passages quoted below suggest that what Marx called a 'productive force' or an 'instrument of labour', determined the nature of the division of labour, the prevailing mode of production and productive relations. (Marx did not always employ these economic categories in a consistent sense.) Sections in *Capital* also give prominence to technology as a historical force.

But if the relations of production (and therefore social and political relations) are determined by handmill and steam-mill, one would expect the transition from antiquity to feudalism to have been accounted for by Marx in terms of a technological innovation. But he mentions none. On the contrary, it was slavery and serfdom – social relations – which distinguished the two epochs according to his own account. Marx also agrees that the industrial revolution of the 18th century came two hundred years after the birth of modern capitalism. The sixth passage quoted below, beginning 'Men never relinquish . . .' emphasises the problem.]

An instrument of labour is a thing, or a complex of things, which the labourer interposes between himself and the subject of his labour, and which serves as the conductor of his activity. He makes use of the mechanical, physical, and chemical properties of some substances in order to make other substances subservient to his aims. Leaving out of consideration such ready-made means of subsistence as fruits, in gathering which a man's own limbs serve as the instruments of his labour, the first thing of which the labourer possesses himself is not the subject of labour but its instrument. Thus Nature becomes one of the organs of his activity, one that he annexes to his own bodily organs, adding stature to himself in spite of the Bible. As the earth is his original larder, so too it is his original tool house. It supplies him, for instance, with stones for throwing, grinding, pressing, cutting, &c. The earth itself is an instrument of labour, but when used as such in agriculture implies a whole series of other instruments and a comparatively high development of labour. No sooner does labour undergo the least development, than it requires specially prepared instruments. Thus in the oldest caves we find stone implements and weapons. In the earliest period of human history domesticated animals, i.e., animals which have been bred for the purpose, and have undergone modifications by means of labour, play the chief part as instruments of labour along with specially prepared stones, wood, bones, and shells. The use and fabrication of instruments of labour, although existing in the germ among certain species of animals, is specifically characteristic of the human labour-process, and Franklin therefore defines man as a tool-making animal. . . .   C.I., p. 179

Machinery is no more an economic category than the bullock that drags the plough. Machinery is merely a productive force. The modern workshop, which depends on the application of machinery, is a social production relation, an economic category.
                                                    P.P., p. 133

Labour is organised, is divided differently according to the instruments it disposes over. The handmill presupposes a different division of labour from the steam-mill. Thus it is slapping history in the face to want to begin by the division of labour in general, in order to get subsequently to a specific instrument of production, machinery.   P.P., p. 133

Social relations are closely bound up with productive forces. In acquiring new productive forces men change their mode of production; and in changing their mode of production, in changing the way of earning their living, they change all their social relations. The handmill gives you society with the feudal lord; the steam-mill, society with the industrial capitalist.

The same men who establish their social relations in conformity with their material productivity, produce also principles, ideas and categories, in conformity with their social relations.

Thus these ideas, these categories, are as little eternal as the relations they express. They are *historical and transitory products*.

There is a continual movement of growth in productive forces, of destruction in social relations, of formation in ideas; the only immutable thing is the abstraction of movement – *mors immortalis*.

P.P., pp. 109–10

Thus the social relations within which individuals produce, *the social relations of production, change, are transformed, with the change and development of the material means of production, the productive forces. The relations of production in their totality constitute what are called the social relations, society, and, specifically, a society at a definite stage of historical development*, a society with a peculiar, distinctive character. *Ancient* society, *feudal* society, *bourgeois* society are such totalities of production relations, each of which at the same time denotes a special stage of development in the history of mankind.

Wage Labour and Capital.   S.W.I., p. 90

B. Pre-Capitalist Society

[Marx's studies of pre-capitalist society were based not on first-hand research but on the conclusions of other authors, notably Maurer and Morgan. The most comprehensive statement of the historical process remains Engels' *The Origin of the Family, Private Property and the State*. However, recently translated notes of Marx dating from 1857–8 considerably enlarge our knowledge of his analysis of pre-capitalist society.

Five epochs emerge: primitive communism, the Asiatic, ancient slavery, feudalism and capitalism. Marx does not insist on the unilinear view that every geographical area must pass through all these stages. But he does suggest a distinct progression in the order given above, in the sense that each stage is in crucial respects further removed from barbarism and historically closer to mature communism.

In classical civilization farming and soldiery go hand in hand. Only landowners are full citizens. Cities are based on landownership. The basic form of labour is slavery. The state unites the cities and protects them against the outside world.]

The first form of ownership is tribal ownership. It corresponds to the undeveloped stage of production, at which a people lives by hunting and fishing, by the rearing of beasts or, in the highest stage, agriculture. In the latter case it presupposes a great mass of uncultivated stretches of land. The division of labour is at this stage still very elementary and is confined to a further extension of the natural division of labour imposed by the family. The social structure is therefore limited to an extension of the family; patriarchal family chieftains; below them the members of the tribe; finally slaves. The slavery latent in the family only develops gradually with the increase of population, the growth of wants, and with the extension of external relations, of war or of trade.

The second form is the ancient communal and State owner-ship which proceeds especially from the union of several tribes into a city by agreement or by conquest, and which is still accompanied by slavery. Beside communal ownership we already find movable, and later also immovable, private property developing, but as an abnormal form subordinate to communal ownership. It is only as a community that the citizens hold power over their labouring slaves, and on this account alone, therefore, they are bound to the form of communal ownership. It is the communal private property which compels the active citizens to remain in this natural form of association over against their slaves. For this reason the whole structure of society based on this communal ownership, and with it the power of the people, decays in the same measure as immovable private property evolves. The division of labour is already more developed. We already find the antagonism of town and country; later the antagonism between those states which repre-sent town interests and those which represent country, and inside the towns themselves the antagonism between industry and maritime commerce. The class relation between citizens and slaves is now completely developed.

This whole interpretation of history appears to be contra-dicted by the fact of conquest. Up till now violence, war, pillage, rape and slaughter, etc. have been accepted as the driving force of history. Here we must limit ourselves to the chief points and take therefore only a striking example – the destruction of an old civilization by a barbarous people and the resulting formation of an entirely new organisation of society. (Rome and the barbarians; Feudalism and Gaul; the Byzantine Empire and the Turks.) With the conquering barbarian people war itself is still, as hinted above, a regular form of intercourse, which is the more eagerly exploited as the population increases, involving the necessity of new means of production to supersede the traditional and, for it, the only possible, crude mode of production. In Italy it was, however, otherwise. The concen-tration of landed property (caused not only by buying-up and indebtedness but also by inheritance, since loose living being rife and marriage rare, the old families died out and their posses-sions fell into the hands of a few) and its conversion into grazing-land (caused not only by economic forces still operative today but by the importation of plundered and tribute-corn and the resultant lack of demand for Italian corn) brought about the almost total disappearance of the free population. The very slaves died out again and again, and had constantly to be replaced by new ones. Slavery remained the basis of the whole productive system. The plebeians, mid-way between freemen and slaves, never succeeded in becoming more than a proletarian rabble. Rome indeed never became more than a city; its connection with the provinces was almost exclusively political and could therefore easily be broken again by political events.

With the development of private property, we find here for the first time the same conditions which we shall find again, only on a more extensive scale, with modern private property. On the one hand the concentration of private property, which began very early in Rome (as the Licinian agrarian law proves), and proceeded very rapidly from the time of the civil wars and especially under the Emperors; on the other hand, coupled with this, the transformation of the plebeian small peasantry into a proletariat, which, however, owing to its intermediate position between propertied citizens and slaves, never achieved an independent development.

The third form of ownership is feudal or estate-property. If antiquity started out from the town and its little territory, the Middle Ages started out from the country. This different starting-point was determined by the sparseness of the population at that time, which was scattered over a large area and which received no large increase from the conquerors. In contrast to Greece and Rome, feudal development therefore extends over a much wider field, prepared by the Roman conquests and the spread of agriculture at first associated with it. The last centuries of the declining Roman Empire and its conquest by the barbarians destroyed a number of productive forces; agriculture had declined, industry had decayed for want of a market, trade had died out or been violently suspended, the rural and urban population had decreased. From these conditions and the mode of organisation of the conquest determined by them, feudal property developed under the influence of the Germanic military constitution. Like tribal and communal ownership, it is based on a community; but the directly producing class standing over against it is not, as in the case of the ancient community, the slaves, but the enserfed small peasantry. As soon as feudalism is fully developed, there also arises antagonisms to the towns. The hierarchical system of land ownership, and the armed bodies of retainers associated with it, gave the nobility power over the serfs. This feudal organisation was, just as much as the ancient communal ownership, an association against a subjected producing class; but the form of association and the relation to the direct producers were different because of the different conditions of production.

This feudal organisation of land-ownership had its counter-part in the towns in the shape of corporative property, the feudal organisation of trades. Here property consisted chiefly in the labour of each individual person. The necessity for associa-tion against the organised robber-nobility, the need for com-munal covered markets in an age when the industrialist was at the same time a merchant, the growing competition of the escaped serfs swarming into the rising towns, the feudal struc-ture of the whole country: these combined to bring about the guilds. Further, the gradually accumulated capital of individual craftsmen and their stable numbers, as against the growing population, evolved the relation of journeyman and apprentice, which brought into being in the towns a hierarchy similar to that in the country.

Thus the chief form of property during the feudal epoch consisted on the one hand of landed property with serf-labour chained to it, and on the other of individual labour with small capital commanding the labour of journeymen. The organisation of both was determined by the restricted conditions of produc-tion – the small-scale and primitive cultivation of the land, and the craft type of industry.

G.I., pp. 9-13

The first prerequisite of this earliest form of landed property appears as a human community, such as emerges from spon-taneous evolution (*naturwüchsig*): the family, the family ex-panded into a tribe, or the tribe created by the inter-marriage of families or combination of tribes. We may take it for granted that pastoralism, or more generally a migratory life, is the first form of maintaining existence, the tribe not settling in a fixed place but using up what it finds locally and then passing on. Men are not settled by nature (unless perhaps in such fertile environments that they could subsist on a single tree like the monkeys; otherwise they would roam, like the wild animals). Hence the tribal community, the natural common body, appears not as the consequence, but as the pre-condition of the joint (temporary) appropriation and use of the soil.

Once men finally settle down, the way in which to a smaller degree this original community is modified, will depend on various external, climatic, geographical, physical, etc., conditions as well as on their special natural make-up – their tribal character. The spontaneously evolved tribal community, or, if you will, the herd – the common ties of blood, language, custom, etc., – is the first precondition of the appropriation of the objective conditions of life, and of the activity which reproduces and gives material expression to, or objectifies (*vergegenständlichenden*) it (activity as herdsmen, hunters, agriculturalists, etc.). The earth is the great laboratory, the arsenal which provides both the means and the materials of labour, and also the location, the *basis* of the community. Men's relation to it is naïve: they regard themselves as its *communal proprietors*, and as those of the community which produces and reproduces itself by living labour. Only in so far as the individual is a member – in the literal and figurative sense – of such a community, does he regard himself as an owner or possessor. In reality *appropriation* by means of the process of labour takes place under these *preconditions*, which are not the *product* of labour but appear as its natural or *divine* preconditions.

Where the fundamental relationship is the same, this form can realise itself in a variety of ways. For instance, as is the case in most Asiatic fundamental forms it is quite compatible with the fact that the *all-embracing unity* which stands above all these small common bodies may appear as the higher or *sole proprietor*, the real communities only as *hereditary* possessors. Since the *unity* is the real owner, and the real precondition of common ownership, it is perfectly possible for it to appear as something separate and superior to the numerous real, particular communities. The individual is then in fact propertyless, or property – i.e. the relationship of the individual to the *natural* conditions of labour and reproduction, the inorganic nature which he finds and makes his own, the objective body of his subjectivity – appears to be mediated by means of a grant (*Ablassen*) from the total unity to the individual through the intermediary of the particular community. The despot here appears as the father of all the numerous lesser communities, thus realising the common unity of all. It therefore follows that the surplus product (which incidentally, is legally determined in terms of [*infolge*] the real appropriation through labour) belongs to this highest unity. Oriental despotism therefore appears to lead to a legal absence of property. In fact, however, its foundation is tribal or common property, in most cases created through a combination of manufacture and agriculture within the small community which thus becomes entirely self-sustaining and contains within itself all conditions of production and surplus production.

Part of its surplus labour belongs to the higher community, which ultimately appears as a *person*. This surplus labour is rendered both as tribute and as common labour for the glory of the unity, in part that of the despot, in part that of the imagined tribal entity of the god. In so far as this type of common property is actually realised in labour, it can appear in two ways. The small communities may vegetate independently side by side, and within each the individual labours independently with his family on the land allotted to him. (There will also be a certain amount of labour for the common store – for insurance as it were – on the one hand; and on the other for defraying the costs of the community as such, i.e. for war, religious worship, etc. The dominion of lords, in its most primitive sense, arises only at this point, e.g. in the Slavonic and Rumanian communities. Here lies the transition to serfdom, etc.) Secondly, the unity can involve a common organisation of labour itself, which in turn can constitute a veritable system, as in Mexico, and especially Peru, among the ancient Celts, and some tribes of India. Furthermore, the communality within the tribal body may tend to appear either as a representation of its unity through the head of the tribal kinship group, or as a relationship between the heads of families. Hence either a more despotic or a more democratic form of the community. The communal conditions for real appropriation through labour, such as irrigation systems (very important among the Asian peoples), means of communication, etc., will then appear as the work of the higher unity – the despotic government which is poised above the lesser communities. Cities in the proper sense arise by the side of these villages only where the location is particularly favourable to external trade, or where the head of the state and his satraps exchange their revenue (the surplus product) against labour, which they expend as labour-funds.

P-C.E.F., pp. 68–71

... The difficulties encountered by the organised community can arise only from other communities which have either already occupied the land or disturb the community in its occupation of it. War is therefore the great all-embracing task, the great communal labour, and it is required either for the occupation of the objective conditions for living existence or for the protection and perpetuation of such occupation. The community, consisting of kinship groups, is therefore in the first instance organised on military lines, as a warlike, military force, and this is one of the conditions of its existence as a proprietor. Concentration of settlement in the city is the foundation of this warlike organisation. The nature of tribal structure leads to the differentiation of kinship groups into higher and lower, and this social differentiation is developed further by the mixing of conquering and conquered tribes, etc. Common land – as state property, *ager publicus* – is here separate from private property. The property of the individual, unlike our first case, is here not direct communal property, where the individual is not an owner in separation from the community, but rather its occupier. Circumstances arise in which individual property does not require communal labour for its valorisation (e.g. as it does in the irrigation systems of the Orient); the purely primitive character of the tribe may be broken by the movement of history or migration; the tribe may remove from its original place of settlement and occupy *foreign* soil, thus entering substantially new conditions of labour and developing the energies of the individual further. The more such factors operate – and the more the communal character of the tribe therefore appears, and must appear, rather as a negative unity as against the outside world – the more do conditions arise which allow the individual to become a *private proprietor* of land – of a particular plot – whose special cultivation belongs to him and his family.

The community – as a state – is, on the one hand, the relationship of these free and equal private proprietors to each other, their combination against the outside world – and at the same time their safeguard. The community is based on the fact that its members consist of working owners of land, small peasant cultivators; but in the same measure the independence of the latter consists in their mutual relation as members of the community, in the safeguarding of the *ager publicus* (common land) for common needs and common glory, etc. To be a member of the community remains the precondition for the appropriation of land, but in his capacity as member of the community the individual is a private proprietor. His relation to his private property is both a relation to the land and to his existence as a member of the community, and his maintenance as a member is the maintenance of the community, and vice versa, etc. Since the community, though it is here not merely a de facto *product of history*, but one of which men are conscious as such, has therefore *had an origin*, we have here the precondition for *property* in land – i.e. for the relation of the working subject to the natural conditions of his labour as belonging to him. . . .

P-C.E.F., pp. 71–73

The Germanic community is not concentrated in the city; a concentration – the city the centre of rural life, the domicile of the land workers, as also the centre of warfare – which gives the community as such an external existence, distinct from that of its individual members. Ancient classical history is the history of cities, but cities based on landownership and agriculture; Asian history is a kind of undifferentiated unity of town and country (the large city, properly speaking, must be regarded merely as a princely camp, superimposed on the real economic structure); the Middle Ages (Germanic period) starts with the countryside as the locus of history, whose further development then proceeds through the opposition of town and country; modern (history) is the urbanisation of the countryside, not, as among the ancients, the ruralisation of the city.

P-C.E.F., pp. 77–78

At bottom every individual household contains an entire economy, forming as it does an independent centre of production (manufacture merely the domestic subsidiary labour of the women, etc.). In classical antiquity the city with its attached territory formed the economic whole, in the Germanic world, the individual home, which itself appears merely as a point in the land belonging to it; there is no concentration of a multiplicity of proprietors, but the family as an independent unit. In the Asiatic form (or at least predominantly so) there is no property, but only individual possession; the community is properly speaking the real proprietor, – hence property only as *communal property* in land. . . .

P-C.E.F., p. 79

[The Asiatic or Oriental mode, according to Marx, is founded on centrally controlled canalisation and other public works. The tribal community forms the basis of a unitary system whose unifying function is represented by the despot. Land is held and tilled in common. It is a static world containing 'all the conditions for reproduction and surplus production within itself'.] There is no ruling class.

The Asiatic form necessarily survives longest and most stubbornly. This is due to the fundamental principle on which it is based, that is, that the individual does not become independent of the community; that the circle of production is self-sustaining, unity of agriculture and craft manufacture, etc. . . .

P-C.E.F., p. 83

If, in a society with capitalist production, anarchy in the social division of labour and despotism in that of the workshop are mutual conditions the one of the other, we find, on the contrary, in those earlier forms of society in which the separation of trades has been spontaneously developed, then crystallised, and finally made permanent by law, on the one hand, a specimen of the organisation of the labour of society, in accordance with an approved and authoritative plan, and on the other, the entire exclusion of division of labour in the workshop, or at all events a mere dwarf-like or sporadic and accidental development of the same.

Those small and extremely ancient Indian communities, some of which have continued down to this day, are based on possession in common of the land, on the blending of agriculture and handicrafts, and on an unalterable division of labour, which serves, whenever a new community is started, as a plan and scheme ready cut and dried. Occupying areas of from 100 up to several thousand acres, each forms a compact whole producing all it requires. The chief part of the products is destined for direct use by the community itself, and does not take the form of a commodity. Hence, production here is independent of that division of labour brought about, in Indian society as a whole, by means of the exchange of commodities. It is the surplus alone that becomes a commodity, and a portion of even that, not until it has reached the hands of the State, into whose hands from time immemorial a certain quantity of these products has found its way in the shape of rent in kind. The constitution of these communities varies in different parts of India. In those of the simplest form, the land is tilled in common, and the produce divided among the members. At the same time, spinning and weaving are carried on in each family as subsidiary industries. Side by side with the masses thus occupied with one and the same work, we find the 'chief inhabitant', who is judge, police, and tax-gatherer in one; the book-keeper, who keeps the accounts of the tillage and registers everything relating thereto; another official, who prosecutes criminals, protects strangers travelling through and escorts them to the next village; the boundary man, who guards the boundaries against neighbouring communities; the water-overseer, who distributes the water from the common tanks for irrigation; the Brahmin, who conducts the religious services; the schoolmaster, who on the sand teaches the children reading and writing; the calendar-Brahmin, or astrologer, who makes known the lucky or unlucky days for seed-time and harvest, and for every other kind of agricultural work; a smith and a carpenter, who make and repair all the agricultural implements; the potter, who makes all the pottery of the village; the barber, the washerman, who washes clothes, the silversmith, here and there the poet, who in some communities replaces the silversmith, in others the schoolmaster. This dozen of individuals is maintained at the expense of the whole community. If the population increases, a new community is founded, on the pattern of the old one, on unoccupied land. The whole mechanism discloses a systematic division of labour; but a division like that in manufactures is impossible, since the smith and the carpenter, &c., find an unchanging market, and at the most there occur, according to the sizes of the villages, two or three of each, instead of one. The law that regulates the division of labour in the community acts with the irresistible authority of a law of Nature, at the same time that each individual artificer, the smith, the carpenter, and so on, conducts in his workshop all the operations of his handicraft in the traditional way, but independently, and without recognising any authority over him. The simplicity of the organisation for production in these self-sufficing communities that constantly reproduce themselves in the same form, and when accidentally destroyed, spring up again on the spot and with the same name – this simplicity supplies the key to the secret of the unchangeableness of Asiatic societies, an unchangeableness in such striking contrast with the constant dissolution and refounding of Asiatic States, and the never-ceasing changes of dynasty. The structure of the economic elements of society remains untouched by the storm-clouds of the political sky. C.I., pp. 356–8

[Feudalism is linked to the decline of classical antiquity. Its social roots, Marx says, lay in the military chieftainships of the barbarian tribes which overran the Roman Empire. The urban population shrank, while perpetual wars forced the independent farmers to seek the protection of an overlord.

This chain of events resembles an accident more than it does a social system evolving dialectically out of the contradictions of the previous one.

Marx seems to have regarded the combination of agrarian]
feudalism and the medieval city as unique to Europe.   ]

... There was little division of labour in the heyday of feudalism. Each land bore in itself the conflict of town and country and the division into estates was certainly strongly marked; but apart from the differentiation of princes, nobility, clergy and peasants in the country, and masters, journeymen, apprentices and soon also the rabble of casual labourers in the towns, no division of importance took place. In agriculture it was rendered difficult by the strip-system, beside which the cottage industry of the peasants themselves emerged as another factor. In industry there was no division of labour at all in the individual trades themselves, and very little between them. The separation of industry and commerce was found already in existence in older towns; in the newer it only developed later, when the towns entered into mutual relations.

The grouping of larger territories into feudal kingdoms was a necessity for the landed nobility as for the towns. The organisation of the ruling class, the nobility, had, therefore, everywhere a monarch at its head.   G.I., p. 13

The greatest division of material and mental labour is the separation of town and country. The antagonism between town and country begins with the transition from barbarism to civilisation, from tribe to State, from locality to nation, and runs through the whole history of civilisation to the present day (the Anti-Corn Law League). The existence of the town implies, at the same time, the necessity of administration, police, taxes, etc., in short, of the municipality, and thus of politics in general. Here first became manifest the division of the population into two great classes, which is directly based on the division of labour and on the instruments of production. The town already is in actual fact the concentration of the population, of the instruments of production, of capital, of pleasures, of needs, while the country demonstrates just the opposite fact, their isolation and separation. The antagonism of town and country can only exist as a result of private property. It is the most crass expression of the subjection of the individual under the division of labour, under a definite activity forced upon him – a subjection which makes one man into a restricted town-animal, the other into a restricted country-animal, and daily creates anew the conflict between their interests. Labour is here again the chief thing, power *over* individuals, and as long as the latter exists, private property must exist. The abolition of the antagonism between town and country is one of the first conditions of communal life, a condition which again depends on a mass of material premises and which cannot be fulfilled by the mere will, as anyone can see at the first glance. (These conditions have still to be enumerated.) The separation of town and country can also be understood as the separation of capital and landed property, as the beginning of the existence and development of capital independent of landed property – the beginning of property having its basis only in labour and exchange.

In the towns, which, in the Middle Ages, did not derive ready-made from an earlier period but were formed anew by the serfs who had become free, each man's own particular labour was his only property apart from the small capital he brought with him, consisting almost solely of the most necessary tools of his craft. The competition of serfs constantly escaping into the town, the constant war of the country against the town and thus the necessity of an organised municipal military force, the bond of common ownership in a particular piece of work, the necessity of common buildings for the sale of their wares at a time when craftsmen were at the same time traders, and the consequent exclusion of the unauthorised from these buildings, the conflict among the interests of the various crafts, the necessity of protecting their laboriously acquired skill, and the feudal organisation of the whole of the country: these were the causes of the union of the workers of each craft in guilds. We have not at this point to go further into the manifold modifications of the guild system, which arise through later historical developments.

The flight of the serfs into the towns went on without interruption right through the Middle Ages. These serfs, persecuted by their lords in the country, came separately into the towns, where they found an organised community, against which they were powerless, in which they had to subject themselves to the station assigned to them by the demand for their labour and the interest of their organised urban competitors. These workers, entering separately, were never able to attain to any power, since if their labour was of the guild type which had to be learned, the guild-masters bent them to their will and organised them according to their interest; or if their labour was not such as had to be learned, and therefore not of the guild type, they became day-labourers and never managed to organise, remaining an unorganised rabble. The need for day-labourers in the towns created the rabble. These towns were true 'associations', called forth by the direct need of providing for the protection of property, and multiplying the means of production and defence of the separate members. The rabble of these towns was devoid of any power, composed as it was of individuals strange to one another who had entered separately, and who stood unorganised over against an organised power, armed for war, and jealously watching over them. The journeymen and apprentices were organised in each craft as it best suited the interest of the masters. The filial relationship in which they stood to their masters gave the latter a double power – on the one hand because of their influence on the whole life of the journeymen, and on the other because, for the journeymen who worked with the same master, it was a real bond, which held them together against the journeymen of other masters and separated them from these. And finally, the journeymen were bound to the existing order by their simple interest in becoming masters themselves. While, therefore, the rabble at least carried out revolts against the whole municipal order, revolts which remained completely ineffective because of their powerlessness, the journeymen never got further than small acts of insubordination within separate guilds, such as belong to the very nature of the guild. The great risings of the Middle Ages all radiated from the country, but equally remained totally ineffective because of the isolation and consequent crudity of the peasants.

G.I., pp. 43–46

[Marx traces the substantial growth of towns to the later middle ages. But he attributes the growth of commercial capital to the great expansion of world trade in the 16th and

17th centuries. Commercial capital became the basis of industrial capital. The rise of capitalism was accompanied by the eclipse of feudal bonds, the waning of sovereign towns and the consolidation of the nation state.

Marx did not, however, demonstrate that feudalism was destined by any inner logic to give birth to capitalism (in the way, for example, that capitalism was to socialism). Once again the dialectical process is obscure.

Money and commodities are not in themselves capital, says Marx. Capitalism cannot flourish until the owners of money and of the means of production confront the mass of dispossessed workers, who are eager to sell their labour power for wages. This dispossessed class, the modern proletariat, is created by the dissolution of feudal ties.

Marx evidently regarded the distinguishing features of capitalism as being: (a) commodity production; (b) surplus-value, and (c) free labour. Only the last was a feature unique to capitalism.

One of the most indispensable conditions for the formation of manufacturing industry was the accumulation of capital, facilitated by the discovery of America and the import of its precious metals.

It is sufficiently proved that the increase in the means of exchange resulted in the depreciation of wages and land rents on the one hand, and the growth of industrial profits on the other. In other words: to the extent that the propertied class and the working class, the feudal lords and the people, sank, to that extent the capitalist class, the bourgeoisie, rose.

There were yet other circumstances which contributed simultaneously to the development of manufacturing industry: the increase of commodities put into circulation from the moment that trade had penetrated to the East Indies by way of the Cape of Good Hope; the colonial system; the development of maritime trade.

Another point which has not yet been sufficiently appreciated in the history of manufacturing industry is the disbanding of the numerous retinues of feudal lords, whose subordinate ranks became vagrants before entering the workshop. The creation of the workshop was preceded by an almost universal vagrancy in the fifteenth and sixteenth centuries. The workshop found, besides, a powerful support in the many peasants who, continually driven from the country owing to the transformation of the fields into pastures and to the progress in agriculture which necessitated fewer hands for the tillage of the soil, went on congregating in the towns during whole centuries.

The growth of the market, the accumulation of capital, the modification in the social position of the classes, a large number of persons being deprived of their sources of income, all these are historical pre-conditions for the formation of manufacture. It was not, as M. Proudhon says, friendly agreements between equals that brought men together into the workshop. It was not even in the bosom of the old guilds that manufacture was born. It was the merchant that became the head of the modern workshop, and not the old guild-master. Almost everywhere there was a desperate struggle between manufacture and crafts.

The accumulation and concentration of instruments and workers preceded the development of the division of labour inside the workshop. Manufacture consisted much more in the bringing together of many workers and many crafts in one place, in one room under the command of one capital, than in the analysis of labour and the adaptation of a special worker to a very simple task.

The utility of a workshop consisted much less in the division of labour as such than in the circumstance that work was done on a much larger scale, that many unnecessary expenses were saved, etc. At the end of the sixteenth and at the beginning of the seventeenth century, Dutch manufacture scarcely knew any division of labour.

The development of the division of labour supposes the assemblage of workers in a workshop. There is not one single example, whether in the sixteenth or in the seventeenth century, of the different branches of one and the same craft being exploited separately to such an extent that it would have sufficed to assemble them all in one place so as to obtain a complete, ready-made workshop. But once the men and the instruments had been brought together, the division of labour, such as it had existed in the form of the guilds, was reproduced, necessarily reflected inside the workshop.   P.P., pp. 136–8

The *original formation of capital* does not, as is often supposed, proceed by the *accumulation* of food, tools, raw materials or in short, of the *objective* conditions of labour detached from the soil and already fused with human labour. Not by means of capital creating the objective conditions of labour. Its *original formation* occurs simply because the historic process of the dissolution of an old mode of production, allows value, existing in the form of *monetary wealth* to *buy* the objective conditions of labour on one hand, to exchange the *living* labour of the now free workers for money, on the other. All these elements are already in existence. What separates them out is a historic process, a process of dissolution, and it is *this* which enables money to turn into *capital*. In so far as money itself plays a part here, it is only to the extent that it is itself an extremely powerful agent of dissolution which intervenes in the process, and hence contributes to the creation of the *plucked*, objective-less, *free labourers*. It is certainly not by *creating* the objective conditions of such labourers' existence, but rather by accelerating their separation from them, i.e. by accelerating their loss of property.

P.C.E.F., p. 110

The genesis of the industrial capitalist did not proceed in such a gradual way as that of the farmer. Doubtless many small guild-masters, and yet more independent small artisans, or even wage-labourers, transformed themselves into small capitalists, and (by gradually extending exploitation of wage-labour and corresponding accumulation) into full-blown capitalists. In the infancy of capitalist production, things often happened as in the infancy of medieval towns, where the question, which of the escaped serfs should be master and which servant, was in great part decided by the earlier or later date of their flight. The snail's pace of this method corresponded in no wise with the commercial requirements of the new world-market that the great discoveries of the end of the 15th century created. But the middle ages had handed down two distinct forms of capital, which mature in the most different economic social formations, and which, before the era of the capitalist mode of production, are considered as capital quand même – usurer's capital and merchant's capital.

The money capital formed by means of usury and commerce was prevented from turning into industrial capital, in the country by the feudal constitution, in the towns by the guild organisation. These fetters vanished with the dissolution of feudal society, with the expropriation and partial eviction of the country population. The new manufactures were established at sea-ports, or at inland points beyond the control of the old municipalities and their guilds. Hence in England an embittered struggle of the corporate towns against these new industrial nurseries.

The discovery of gold and silver in America, the extirpation, enslavement and entombment in mines of the aboriginal population, the beginning of the conquest and looting of the East Indies, the turning of Africa into a warren for the commercial hunting of black-skins, signalised the rosy dawn of the era of capitalist production. These idyllic proceedings are the chief momenta of primitive accumulation. On their heels treads the commercial war of the European nations, with the globe for a theatre. It begins with the revolt of the Netherlands from Spain, assumes giant dimensions in England's Anti-Jacobin War, and is still going on in the opium wars against China, &c.

The different momenta of primitive accumulation distribute themselves now, more or less in chronological order, particularly over Spain, Portugal, Holland, France, and England. In England at the end of the 17th century, they arrive at a systematical combination, embracing the colonies, the national debt, the modern mode of taxation, and the protectionist system. These methods depend in part on brute force, e.g., the colonial system. But they all employ the power of the State, the concentrated and organised force of society, to hasten, hot house fashion, the process of transformation of the feudal mode of production into the capitalist mode, and to shorten the transition. Force is the midwife of every old society pregnant with a new one. It is itself an economic power.   C.I., pp. 750–1

The colonial system ripened, like a hot-house, trade and navigation. The 'societies Monopolia' of Luther were powerful levers for concentration of capital. The colonies secured a market for the budding manufactures, and, through the monopoly of the market, an increased accumulation. The treasures captured outside Europe by undisguised looting, enslavement, and murder, floated back to the mother-country, and were there turned into capital. Holland, which first fully developed the colonial system, in 1648 stood already in the acme of its commercial greatness. . . .

Today industrial supremacy implies commercial supremacy. In the period of manufacture properly so called, it is, on the other hand, the commercial supremacy that gives industrial predominance. Hence the preponderant role that the colonial system plays at that time. . . . C.I., pp. 753–4

The first distinction we notice between money that is money only, and money that is capital, is nothing more than a difference in their form of circulation.

The simplest form of the circulation of commodities is C-M-C, the transformation of commodities into money, and the change of the money back again into commodities; or selling in order to buy. But alongside of this form we find another specifically different form: M-C-M, the transformation of money into commodities, and the change of commodities back again into money; or buying in order to sell. Money that circulates in the latter manner is thereby transformed into, becomes capital, and is already potentially capital.

C.I., pp. 146–7

The conversion of a sum of money into means of production and labour-power, is the first step taken by the quantum of value that is going to function as capital. This conversion takes place in the market, within the sphere of circulation. The second step, the process of production, is complete so soon as the means of production have been converted into commodities whose value exceeds that of their component parts, and, therefore, contains the capital originally advanced, plus a surplus-value. These commodities must then be thrown into circulation. They must be sold, their value realised in money, this money afresh converted into capital, and so over and over again. This circular movement, in which the same phases are continually gone through in succession, forms the circulation of capital.

C.I., p. 564

As the conscious representative of this movement, the possessor of money becomes a capitalist. His person, or rather his pocket, is the point from which the money starts and to which it returns. The expansion of value, which is the objective basis or main-spring of the circulation M-C-M, becomes his subjective aim, and it is only in so far as the appropriation of ever more and more wealth in the abstract becomes the sole motive of his operations, that he functions as a capitalist, that is, as capital personified and endowed with consciousness and a will. Use-values must therefore never be looked upon as the real aim of the capitalist; neither must the profit on any single transaction. The restless never-ending process of profit-making alone is what he aims at. This boundless greed after riches, this passionate chase after exchange-value, is common to the capitalist and the miser; but while the miser is merely a capitalist gone mad, the capitalist is a rational miser. The never-ending augmentation of exchange-value, which the miser strives after, by seeking to save his money from circulation, is attained by the more acute capitalist, by constantly throwing it afresh into circulation.   C.I., pp. 152–3

This competition has the further consequence that a large part of landed property falls into the hands of the capitalists and that capitalists thus become simultaneously landowners, just as the smaller landowners, are on the whole already nothing more than capitalists. Similarly, a section of large landowners become simultaneously industrialists.

The final consequence is thus the abolishment of the distinction between capitalist and landowner, so that there remain altogether only two classes of the population – the working class and the class of capitalists. This huckstering with landed property, the transformation of landed property into a commodity, constitutes the final overthrow of the old and the final consummation of the money aristocracy.

                                        E.P.M., pp. 60–61

[In view of the fact that the Marxist-Communist revolution came first to peasant Russia, rather than to the capitalist West, Marx's statements about Russia (he learned Russian in order to study the situation there) are of great interest. They certainly dispose of any unilinear philosophy of history, and they suggest that Marx did not insist that socialism must be the child of mature capitalism. The Russian 'mir' or commune, a primitive socialist agrarian organisation, offered an alternative starting point. Marx was clearly very uncertain about this, and in the light of his general theory he had cause to be. Later Russian Marxists, both Bolsheviks and Mensheviks, rightly based their policies on the assumption that Russia was already beginning to pass through the capitalist epoch.

The Communist Manifesto had as its object the proclamation of the inevitably impending dissolution of modern bourgeois property. But in Russia we find, face to face with the rapidly developing capitalist swindle and bourgeois landed property, just beginning to develop, more than half the land owned in common by the peasants. Now the question is: can the Russian *obshchina*, though greatly undermined, yet a form of the primeval common ownership of land, pass directly to the higher form of communist common ownership? Or on the contrary, must it first pass through the same process of dissolution as constitutes the historical evolution of the West?

The only answer to that possible today is this: If the Russian Revolution becomes the signal for a proletarian revolution in the West, so that both complement each other, the present Russian common ownership of land may serve as the starting point for a communist development.

C.M., pp. 13–14

Preface to the Russian edition of 1882
In analysing the genesis of capitalist production I say:

'The foundation of the capitalist system is therefore the utmost separation of the producer from the means of production . . . The basis of this whole development is the *expropriation of the agricultural producer*. This has been accomplished in radical fashion only in England . . . But *all the countries of Western Europe* are going through the same movement.' (*Capital*, French ed., p. 315).

Hence the 'historical inevitability' of this movement is *expressly* limited to the *countries of Western Europe*. The reason for this limitation is indicated in the following passage of Chapter XXXII:

'*Self-earned private property* . . . will be supplanted by *capitalistic private property*, which rests on the exploitation of the labour of others, on wages-labour.' (*Ibid.*, p. 341.)

In this western movement the point in question therefore is the *transformation of one form of private property into another form of private property*. With the Russian peasants one would on the contrary have to *transform their common property into private property*.

Thus the analysis given in *Capital* assigns no reasons for or against the vitality of the rural community, but the special research into this subject which I conducted, the materials which I obtained from original sources, has convinced me that this community is the mainspring of Russia's social regeneration, but in order that it might function as such one would first have to eliminate the deleterious influences which assail it from every quarter and then to ensure the conditions normal for spontaneous development.

Marx to V. I. Zasulich, March 8, 1881.   S.C., p. 412

C. Labour

[After 1850 Marx devoted the greater part of his energies to the analysis of capitalism itself. Capitalism inherits from pre-capitalist society the division of labour, which we have already encountered as the basis of human alienation and of the class-divided society.]

Division of labour and *exchange* are the two *phenomena* in connection with which the political economist boasts of the social character of his science and in the same breath gives expression to the contradiction in his science – the establishment of society through unsocial, particular interests.

E.P.M., p. 135

The division of labour inside a nation leads at first to the separation of industrial and commercial from agricultural labour, and hence to the separation of town and country and a clash of interests between them. Its further development leads to the separation of commercial from industrial labour. At the same time through the division of labour there develop further, inside these various branches, various divisions among the individuals co-operating in definite kinds of labour. The relative position of these individual groups is determined by the methods employed in agriculture, industry and commerce (patriarchalism, slavery, estates, classes). These same conditions are to be seen (given a more developed intercourse) in the relations of different nations to one another.

The various stages of development in the division of labour are just so many different forms of ownership; i.e. the existing stage in the division of labour determines also the relations of individuals to one another with reference to the material, instrument, and product of labour.

G.I., pp. 8–9

With the division of labour, in which all these contradictions are implicit, and which in its turn is based on the natural division of labour in the family and the separation of society into individual families opposed to one another, is given simultaneously the distribution, and indeed the unequal distribution, (both quantitative and qualitative), of labour and its products, hence property: the nucleus, the first form, of which lies in the family, where wife and children are the slaves of the husband. This latent slavery in the family, though still very crude, is the first property, but even at this early stage it corresponds perfectly to the definition of modern economists who call it the power of disposing of the labour-power of others. Division of labour and private property are, moreover, identical expressions: in the one the same thing is affirmed with reference to activity as is affirmed in the other with reference to the product of the activity.

G.I., pp. 21–22

Society as a whole has this in common with the interior of a workshop, that it too has its division of labour. If one took as a model the division of labour in a modern workshop, in order to apply it to a whole society, the society best organised for the production of wealth would undoubtedly be that which had a single chief employer, distributing tasks to the different members of the community according to a previously fixed rule. But this is by no means the case. While inside the modern workshop the division of labour is meticulously regulated by the authority of the employer, modern society has no other rule, no other authority for the distribution of labour than free competition.

Under the patriarchal system, under the caste system, under the feudal and corporative system, there was division of labour in the whole of society according to fixed rules. Were these rules established by a legislator? No. Originally born of the conditions of material production, they were raised to the status of laws only much later. In this way these different forms of the division of labour became so many bases of social organisation. As for the division of labour in the workshop, it was very little developed in all these forms of society.

It can even be laid down as a general rule that the less authority presides over the division of labour inside society, the more the division of labour develops inside the workshop, and the more it is subjected there to the authority of a single person. Thus authority in the workshop and authority in society, in relation to the division of labour, are in *inverse ratio* to each other.

P.P., pp. 135–6

Division of labour in a society, and the corresponding tying down of individuals to a particular calling, develops itself, just as does the division of labour in manufacture, from opposite starting-points. Within a family, and after further development within a tribe, there springs up naturally a division of labour, caused by differences of sex and age, a division that is consequently based on a purely physiological foundation, which division enlarges its materials by the expansion of the community, by the increase of population, and more especially, by the conflicts between different tribes, and the subjugation of one tribe by another. On the other hand, as I have before remarked, the exchange of products springs up at the points where different families, tribes, communities, come in contact; for, in the beginning of civilisation, it is not private individuals but families, tribes, &c., that meet on an independent footing. Different communities find different means of production, and different means of subsistence in their natural environment. Hence, their modes of production, and of living, and their products are different. It is this spontaneously developed difference which, when different communities come into contact, calls forth the mutual exchange of products, and the consequent gradual conversion of those products into commodities. Exchange does not create the differences between the spheres of production, but brings what are already different into relation, and thus converts them into more or less interdependent branches of the collective production of an enlarged society. In the latter case, the social division of labour arises from the exchange between spheres of production, that are originally distinct and independent of one another. In the former, where the physiological division of labour is the starting-point, the particular organs of a compact whole grow loose, and break off, principally owing to the exchange of commodities with foreign communities, and then isolate themselves so far, that the sole bond, still connecting the various kinds of work, is the exchange of the products as commodities. In the one case, it is the making dependent what was before independent; in the other case, the making independent what was before dependent.

The foundation of every division of labour that is well developed, and brought about by the exchange of commodities, is the separation between town and country. It may be said, that the whole economic history of society is summed up in the movement of this antithesis. . . .

C.I., pp. 351–2

The greater *division of labour* enables *one* worker to do the work of five, ten or twenty; it therefore multiplies competition among the workers fivefold, tenfold and twentyfold. The workers do not only compete by one selling himself cheaper than another; they compete by *one* doing the work of five, ten, twenty; and the *division of labour*, introduced by capital and continually increased, compels the workers to compete among themselves in this way.

Further, as the *division of labour* increases, labour is *simplified*. The special skill of the worker becomes worthless. He becomes transformed into a simple, monotonous productive force that does not have to use intense bodily or intellectual faculties. His labour becomes a labour that anyone can perform. . . .

Therefore, as labour becomes more unsatisfying, more repulsive, competition increases and wages decrease. The worker tries to keep up the amount of his wages by working more, whether by working longer hours or by producing more in one hour.

Driven by want, therefore, he still further increases the evil effects of the division of labour. The result is that *the more he works the less wages he receives*, and for the simple reason that he competes to that extent with his fellow workers, hence makes them into so many competitors who offer themselves on just the same bad terms as he does himself, and that, therefore, in the last resort he *competes with himself, with himself as a member of the working class.*

Machinery brings about the same results on a much greater scale, by replacing skilled workers by unskilled, men by women, adults by children. It brings about the same results, where it is newly introduced, by throwing the hand workers on to the streets in masses, and, where it is developed, improved and replaced by more productive machinery, by discharging workers in smaller batches. . . .

Wage Labour and Capital. S.W.I., pp. 102–3

The concentration of the instruments of production and the division of labour are as inseparable one from the other as are, in the political sphere, the concentration of public authority and the division of private interests. England, with the concentration of the land, this instrument of agricultural labour, has at the same time division of agricultural labour and the application of machinery to the exploitation of the soil. France, which has the division of the instruments, the small holdings system, has, in general, neither division of agricultural labour nor application of machinery to the soil.

For M. Proudhon the concentration of the instruments of labour is the negation of the division of labour. In reality we find again the reverse. As the concentration of instruments develops, the division develops also, and *vice versa*. This is why every big mechanical invention is followed by a greater division of labour, and each increase in the division of labour gives rise in turn to new mechanical inventions.

We need not recall the fact that the great progress of the division of labour began in England after the invention of machinery. Thus the weavers and spinners were for the most part peasants like those one still meets in backward countries.

The invention of machinery brought about the separation of manufacturing industry from agricultural industry. The weaver and the spinner, united but lately in a single family, were separated by the machine. Thanks to the machine, the spinner can live in England while the weaver resides in the East Indies. Before the invention of machinery, the industry of a country was carried on chiefly with raw materials that were the products of its own soil; in England – wool, in Germany – flax, in France – silks and flax, in the East Indies and the Levant – cotton, etc. Thanks to the application of machinery and of steam, the division of labour was able to assume such dimensions that large-scale industry, detached from the national soil, depends entirely on the world market, on international exchange, on an international division of labour. In short – the machine has so great an influence on the division of labour, that when, in the manufacture of some object, a means has been found to produce parts of it mechanically, the manufacture splits up immediately into two works independent of each other.

When in England the market had become so far developed that manual labour was no longer adequate, the need for machinery was felt. Then came the idea of the application of mechanical science, already quite developed in the eighteenth century.

The automatic workshop opened its career with acts which were anything but philanthropic. Children were kept at work at the whip's end; they were made an object of traffic and contracts were undertaken with the orphanages. All the laws on the apprenticeship of workers were repealed, because, to use M. Proudhon's phraseology, there was no further need of *synthetic* workers. Finally, from 1825 onwards, almost all the new inventions were the result of collisions between the worker and the employer who sought at all costs to depreciate the worker's specialized ability. After each new strike of any importance, there appeared a new machine. So little indeed did the worker see in the application of machinery a sort of rehabilitation, *restoration* – as M. Proudhon would say – that in the eighteenth century he stood out for a very long time against the incipient domination of the automaton.

P.P., pp. 139-40

Let us sum up: *The more productive capital grows, the more the division of labour and the application of machinery expands. The more the division of labour and the application of machinery expands, the more competition among the workers expands and the more their wages contract.*

Wage Labour and Capital. S.W.I., p. 104

[Capitalism feeds on free labour. 'It consists of living labour serving accumulated labour as a means of maintaining and multiplying the exchange value of the latter.']

The serf belongs to the land and turns over to the owner of the land the fruits thereof. The *free labourer*, on the other hand, sells himself and, indeed, sells himself piecemeal. He sells at auction eight, ten, twelve, fifteen hours of his life, day after day, to the highest bidder, to the owner of the raw materials, instruments of labour and means of subsistence, that is, to the capitalist. The worker belongs neither to an owner nor to the land, but eight, ten, twelve, fifteen hours of his daily life belong to him who buys them. The worker leaves the capitalist to whom he hires himself whenever he likes, and the capitalist discharges him whenever he thinks fit, as soon as he no longer gets any profit out of him, or not the anticipated profit. But the worker whose sole source of livelihood is the sale or his labour power, cannot leave the *whole class of purchasers, that is, the capitalist class*, without renouncing his existence. He belongs not to this or that capitalist but to the *capitalist class*, and, moreover, it is his business to dispose of himself, that is, to find a purchaser within this capitalist class.

Wage Labour and Capital. S.W.I., p. 83

How, then does any amount of commodities, of exchange value, become capital?

By maintaining and multiplying itself as an independent social *power*, that is, as the power *of a portion of society*, by means of its *exchange for direct, living labour power.* The existence of a class which possesses nothing but its capacity to labour is a necessary prerequisite of capital.

It is only the domination of accumulated past, materialised labour over direct, living labour that turns accumulated labour into capital.

Capital does not consist in accumulated labour serving living labour as a means for new production. It consists in living labour serving accumulated labour as a means for maintaining and multiplying the exchange value of the latter.

What takes place in the exchange between capitalist and wage-worker?

Wage Labour and Capital.   S.W.I., p. 91

'What is a working-day? What is the length of t..ne during which capital may consume the labour-power whose daily value it buys? How far may the working-day be extended beyond the working-time necessary for the reproduction of labour-power itself?' It has been seen that to these questions capital replies: the working-day contains the full 24 hours, with the deduction of the few hours of repose without which labour-power absolutely refuses its services again. Hence it is self-evident that the labourer is nothing else, his whole life through, than labour-power, that therefore all his disposable time is by nature and law labour-time, to be devoted to the self-expansion of capital. Time for education, for intellectual development, for the fulfilling of social functions and for social intercourse, for the free-play of his bodily and mental activity, even the rest time of Sunday (and that in a country of Sabbatarians!) – moonshine! But in its blind unrestrainable passion, its werewolf hunger for surplus labour, capital oversteps not only the moral, but even the merely physical maximum bounds of the working-day. It usurps the time for growth, development, and healthy maintenance of the body. It steals the time required for the consumption of fresh air and sunlight. It higgles over a meal-time, incorporating it where possible with the process of production itself, so that food is given to the labourer as to a mere means of production, as coal is supplied to the boiler, grease and oil to the machinery.

It reduces the sound sleep needed for the restoration, reparation, refreshment of the bodily powers to just so many hours of torpor as the revival of an organism, absolutely exhausted, renders essential. It is not the normal maintenance of the labour-power which is to determine the limits of the working-day; it is the greatest possible daily expenditure of labour-power, no matter how diseased, compulsory, and painful it may be, which is to determine the limits of the labourers' period of repose. Capital cares nothing for the length of life of labour-power. All that concerns it is simply and solely the maximum of labour-power, that can be rendered fluent in a working-day. It attains this end by shortening the extent of the labourer's life, as a greedy farmer snatches increased produce from the soil by robbing it of its fertility.   C.I., pp. 264–5

Capital is thus the *governing power* over labour and its products. The capitalist possesses this power, not on account of his personal or human qualities, but inasmuch as he is an *owner* of capital. His power is the *purchasing* power of his capital, which nothing can withstand.

Later we shall see first how the capitalist, by means of capital, exercises his governing power over labour, then, however, we shall see the governing power of capital over the capitalist himself.

What is capital?

Capital is *stored-up labour*.

E.P.M., pp. 36–37

Capital can only increase by exchanging itself for labour power, by calling wage labour to life. The labour power of the wage-worker can only be exchanged for capital by increasing capital, by strengthening the power whose slave it is. *Hence, increase of capital is increase of the proletariat, that is, of the working class.*

Wage Labour and Capital.   S.W.I., p. 92

[No aspect of Marx's theory has been more hotly challenged than his theories of wage levels, value and surplus value. Marx argued that the basic wage is determined by the cost of maintaining the worker and his family at subsistence level – in other words, by the cost of the maintenance and reproduction of labour. Marx inherited this theory from the 'classical' British economists David Ricardo and Adam Smith. He acknowledged that the market price of labour fluctuates with supply and demand, but he insisted that in the long run the market price (i.e. wages), like the price of other commodities, adapts itself to the value of the labour – which is in turn based on the cost of maintaining labour at subsistence level. In order to get round the logical difficulty of defining the value of labour in terms of labour itself, Marx and Engels later substituted the formula 'labour-power' for 'labour'. Thus it became a question of the amount of actual labour required to produce the goods which kept alive labour-power, i.e. the worker.

Marx added that the value of labour in each country is partly determined by traditional standards of living.]

The separation of capital, ground-rent and labour is thus fatal for the worker.

The lowest and the only necessary wage-rate is that providing for the subsistence of the worker for the duration of his work and as much more as is necessary for him to support a family and for the race of labourers not to die out. The ordinary wage, according to Smith,* is the lowest compatible with common humanity (that is, a cattle-like existence).

E.P.M., p. 21

As the landlord can demand all the more rent from the tenant farmer the less wages the farmer pays, and as the farmer forces down wages all the lower the more rent the landlord demands, it follows that the interest of the landlord is just as hostile to that of the farm workers as is that of the manufacturers to their

* Adam Smith, author of the 'Wealth of Nations' and regarded by Marx as a prophet of laissez-faire capitalism.

workers. It forces down wages to the minimum in just the same way.

Since a real reduction in the price of manufactured products raises the rent of land, the landowner has a direct interest in lowering the wages of industrial workers, in competition amongst the capitalists, in over-production, in all the misery associated with industrial production.

E.P.M., p. 58

To sum up: Labour, being itself a commodity, is measured as such by the labour time needed to produce the labour-commodity. And what is needed to produce this labour-commodity? Just enough labour time to produce the objects indispensable to the constant maintenance of labour, that is, to keep the worker alive and in a condition to propagate his race. The natural price of labour is no other than the wage minimum.

P.P., p. 51

Owing to the extensive use of machinery and to division of labour, the work of the proletarians has lost all individual character, and, consequently, all charm for the workman. He becomes an appendage of the machine, and it is only the most simple, most monotonous, and most easily acquired knack, that is required of him. Hence, the cost of production of a workman is restricted, almost entirely, to the means of subsistence that he requires for his maintenance, and for the propagation of his race. But the price of a commodity, and therefore also of labour, is equal to its cost of production. In proportion, therefore, as the repulsiveness of the work increases, the wage decreases. Nay more, in proportion as the use of machinery and division of labour increases, in the same proportion the burden of toil also increases, whether by prolongation of the working hours, by increase of the work exacted in a given time or by increased speed of the machinery, etc.

Modern industry has converted the little workshop of the patriarchal master into the great factory of the industrial capitalist. Masses of labourers, crowded into the factory, are organised like soldiers. As privates of the industrial army they are placed under the command of a perfect hierarchy of officers and sergeants. Not only are they slaves of the bourgeois class, and of the bourgeois State; they are daily and hourly enslaved by the machine, by the over-looker, and, above all, by the individual bourgeois manufacturer himself. The more openly this despotism proclaims gain to be its end and aim, the more petty, the more hateful and the more embittering it is.

C.M., pp. 57–59

[Marx later abandoned the idea that the worker sells his labour to the capitalist, and substituted the formula 'labour-power'. In the passage which follows, dating from 1847, Engels has changed Marx's original phrasing in this single respect.]

The determination of price by the cost of production is equivalent to the determination of price by the labour time necessary for the manufacture of a commodity, for the cost of production consists of 1) raw materials and depreciation of instruments, that is, of industrial products the production of which has cost a certain amount of labour days and which, therefore, represent a certain amount of labour time, and 2) of direct labour, the measure of which is, precisely, time.

Now, the same general laws that regulate the price of commodities in general of course also regulate *wages*, the *price of labour*.

Wages will rise and fall according to the relation of supply and demand, according to the turn taken by the competition between the buyers of labour power, the capitalists, and the sellers of labour power, the workers. The fluctuations in wages correspond in general to the fluctuations in prices of commodities. *Within these fluctuations, however, the price of labour will be determined by the cost of production, by the labour time necessary to produce this commodity – labour power.*

What, then, is the cost of production of labour power?

It is the cost required for maintaining the worker as a worker and of developing him into a worker.

The less the period of training, therefore, that any work requires the smaller is the cost of production of the worker and the lower is the price of his labour, his wages. In those branches of industry in which hardly any period of apprenticeship is required and where the mere bodily existence of the worker suffices, the cost necessary for his production is almost confined to the commodities necessary for keeping him alive and capable of working. The *price of his labour* will, therefore, be determined by the *price of the necessary means of subsistence.*

Another consideration, however, also comes in. The manufacturer in calculating his cost of production and, accordingly, the price of the products takes into account the wear and tear of the instruments of labour. If, for example, a machine costs him 1,000 marks and wears out in ten years, he adds 100 marks annually to the price of the commodities so as to be able to replace the worn-out machine by a new one at the end of ten years. In the same way, in calculating the cost of production of simple labour power, there must be included the cost of reproduction, whereby the race of workers is enabled to multiply and to replace worn-out workers by new ones. Thus the depreciation of the worker is taken into account in the same way as the depreciation of the machine.

The cost of production of simple labour, therefore, amounts to the *cost of existence and reproduction of the worker.* The price of this cost of existence and reproduction constitutes wages. Wages so determined are called the *wage minimum.* This wage minimum, like the determination of the price of commodities by the cost of production in general, does not hold good for the *single individual* but for the *species.* Individual workers, millions of workers, do not get enough to be able to exist and reproduce themselves; *but the wages of the whole working class* level down, within their fluctuations, to this minimum.

Wage Labour and Capital. S.W.I., pp. 87–89

What the working man sells is not directly his *Labour*, but his *Labouring Power*, the temporary disposal of which he makes over to the capitalist. . . .

Wages, Price and Profit. S.W.I., p. 424

By labour-power or capacity for labour is to be understood the aggregate of those mental and physical capabilities existing in a human being, which he exercises whenever he produces a use-value of any description.   C.I., p. 167

What, then, is the *Value of Labouring Power?*

Like that of every other commodity, its value is determined by the quantity of labour necessary to produce it. The labouring power of a man exists only in his living individuality. A certain mass of necessaries must be consumed by a man to grow up and maintain his life. But the man, like the machine, will wear out, and must be replaced by another man. Beside the mass of necessaries required for *his own* maintenance, he wants another amount of necessaries to bring up a certain quota of children that are to replace him on the labour market and to perpetuate the race of labourers. Moreover, to develop his labouring power, and acquire a given skill, another amount of values must be spent. For our purpose it suffices to consider only *average* labour, the costs of whose education and development are vanishing magnitudes. Still I must seize upon this occasion to state that, as the costs of producing labouring powers of different quality differ, so must differ the values of the labouring powers employed in different trades. The cry for an *equality of wages* rests, therefore, upon a mistake, is an *insane* wish never to be fulfilled. It is an offspring of that false and superficial radicalism that accepts premises and tries to evade conclusions. Upon the basis of the wages system the value of labouring power is settled like that of every other commodity; and as different kinds of labouring power have different values, or require different quantities of labour for their production, they *must* fetch different prices in the labour market. To clamour for *equal or even equitable retribution* on the basis of the wages system is the same as to clamour for *freedom* on the basis of the slavery system. What you think just or equitable is out of the question. The question is: What is necessary and unavoidable with a given system of production?

After what has been said, it will be seen that the *value of labouring power* is determined by the *value of the necessaries* required to produce, develop, maintain, and perpetuate the labouring power.

Wages, Price and Profit. S.W.I., pp. 425–6

[According to Marx, the main purpose of the capitalist is 'to extract the greatest possible amount of surplus-value, and consequently to exploit labour-power to the greatest possible extent'. Marx leaves no doubt as to what he means by surplus-value. It consists of unpaid labour. It can be increased either by prolonging the working day (absolute surplus value), or alternatively by curtailing the time necessary to manufacture a commodity (relative surplus value).

Defining labour as variable capital, Marx calls the ratio of surplus value to variable capital the rate of exploitation. A reduction in the length of the working day need not reduce the rate of exploitation, because new machines may extract more labour in a given time.

Marx believed that machinery, by bringing the whole family on to the labour market, necessarily reduced the value of labour-power. This was not because the supply of labour became more plentiful, but because the maintenance of a single family now produced (say) four pairs of labouring hands instead of only one.]

Now suppose that the average amount the of daily necessaries of a labouring man require *six hours of average labour* for their production. Suppose, moreover, six hours of average labour to be also realised in a quantity of gold equal to 3s. Then 3s. would be the *Price*, or the monetary expression of the *Daily Value* of that man's *Labouring Power*. If he worked daily six hours he would daily produce a value sufficient to buy the average amount of his daily necessaries, or to maintain himself as a labouring man.

But our man is a wages labourer. He must, therefore, sell his labouring power to a capitalist. If he sells it at 3s. daily, or 18s. weekly, he sells it at its value. Suppose him to be a spinner. If he works six hours daily he will add to the cotton a value of 3s. daily. This value, daily added by him, would be an exact equivalent for the wages, or the price of his labouring power, received daily. But in that case *no surplus value or surplus produce* whatever would go to the capitalist. Here, then, we come to the rub.

... The quantity of labour by which the *value* of the workman's labouring power is limited forms by no means a limit to the quantity of labour which his labouring power is apt to perform. Take the example of our spinner. We have seen that, to daily reproduce his labouring power, he must daily reproduce a value of three shillings, which he will do by working six hours daily. But this does not disable him from working ten or twelve or more hours a day. But by paying the daily or weekly *value* of the spinner's labouring power, the capitalist has acquired the right of using that labouring power during *the whole day or week*. He will, therefore, make him work say, daily, *twelve* hours. *Over and above* the six hours required to replace his wages, or the value of his labouring power, he will, therefore, have to work *six other hours*, whidh I shall call hours of *surplus labour*, which surplus labour will realise itself in a *surplus value* and a *surplus produce*. ... By repeating this same process daily, the capitalist will daily advance three shillings and daily pocket six shillings, one-half of which will go to pay wages anew, and the other half of which will form *surplus value*, for which the capitalist pays no equivalent. It is this *sort of exchange between capital and labour* upon which capitalistic production, or the wages system, is founded, and which must constantly result in reproducing the working man as a working man, and the capitalist as a capitalist.

The rate of surplus value, all other circumstances remaining the same, will depend on the proportion between that part of the working day necessary to reproduce the value of the labouring power and the *surplus time* or *surplus labour* performed for the capitalist. It will, therefore, depend on the *ratio in which the working day is prolonged over and above that extent*, by working which the working man would only reproduce the value of his labouring power, or replace his wages.

Wages, Price and Profit. S.W.I., pp. 426–8

On these assumptions the value of labour-power, and the magnitude of surplus-value, are determined by three laws.

(1) A working-day of given length always creates the same amount of value, no matter how the productiveness of labour, and, with it, the mass of the product, and the price of each single commodity produced, may vary.

If the value created by a working-day of 12 hours be, say, six shillings, then, although the mass of the articles produced varies with the productiveness of labour, the only result is that the value represented by six shillings is spread over a greater or less number of articles.

(2) Surplus-value and the value of labour-power vary in opposite directions. A variation in the productiveness of labour, its increase or diminution, causes a variation in the opposite direction in the value of labour-power, and in the same direction in surplus-value.

(3) Increase or diminution in surplus-value is always consequent on, and never the cause of, the corresponding diminution or increase in the value of labour-power.

C.I., p. 520 & p. 522

The value of labour-power was determined, not only by the labour-time necessary to maintain the individual adult labourer, but also by that necessary to maintain his family. Machinery, by throwing every member of that family on to the labour-market, spreads the value of the man's labour-power over his whole family. It thus depreciates his labour-power. To purchase the labour-power of a family of four workers may, perhaps, cost more than it formerly did to purchase the labour power of the head of the family, but, in return, four days' labour takes the place of one, and their price falls in proportion to the excess of surplus-labour of four over the surplus-labour of one. In order that the family may live, four people must now, not only labour, but expend surplus-labour for the capitalist. Thus we see, that machinery, while augmenting the human material that forms the principal object of capital's exploiting power, at the same time raises the degree of exploitation. C.I., p. 395

D. Value – Profit – Price

[Many people would find it hard to distinguish between value and price. Ricardo regarded the two as synonymous. Marx did not. He denied that value was determined by supply and demand. He took labour as the measure of value. The value of a commodity was to be measured by the quantity of labour-time embodied in it. However, he made some qualifications.

Nothing could have value without being in social demand. Marx did not concede that market fluctuations in demand determined social utility, but spoke instead of what was in the long run 'socially necessary' (surely a nebulous concept). Nor did he regard all labour as productive of value. He excluded the labour of the capitalist, the banker and the merchant. This suggests that his theory of value was not simply, as he claimed, 'the scientific expression of economic relations of present-day society', but was also a moral theory.

But supposing one worker produces more in an hour than another? How then can the value of a commodity be measured by the quantity of labour-time embodied in it? Marx falls back on the formula 'socially necessary labour time' under average conditions of production.

In the passage which follows Marx quotes from Ricardo's *Principles of Political Economy*, to which his theory of value owes much.]

'Economy in the use of labour never fails to reduce the relative value of a commodity, whether the saving be in the labour necessary to the manufacture of the commodity itself, or in that necessary to the formation of the capital by the aid of which it is produced.' 'Under such circumstances the value of the deer, the produce of the hunter's day's labour, would be exactly equal to the value of the fish, the produce of the fisherman's day's labour. The comparative value of the fish and the game, would be entirely regulated by the quantity of labour realised in each; whatever might be the quantity of production, or however high or low general wages or profits might be '. 'In making labour the foundation of the value of commodities and the comparative quantity of labour which is necessary to their production, the rule which determines the respective quantities of goods which shall be given in exchange for each other, we must not be supposed to deny the accidental and temporary deviations of the actual or market price of commodities from this, their primary and natural price '. 'It is the cost of production which must ultimately regulate the price of commodities and not, as has been often said, the proportion between supply and demand.' P.P., pp. 47–48

Let us suppose for a moment that a jeweller's day is equivalent to three days of a weaver; the fact remains that any change in the value of jewels relative to that of woven materials, unless it be the transitory result of the fluctuations of supply and demand, must have as its cause a reduction or an increase in the labour time expended in the production of one or the other. If three working days of different workers be related to one another in the ratio of $1 : 2 : 3$, then every change in the relative value of their products will be a change in this same proportion of $1 : 2 : 3$. Thus values can be measured by labour time, in spite of the inequality of value of different working days; but to apply such a measure we must have a comparative scale of the different working days: it is competition that sets up this scale.

Is your hour's labour worth mine? That is a question which is decided by competition.

Competition, according to an American economist, determines how many days of simple labour are contained in one day's compound labour. Does this reduction of days of compound labour to days of simple labour suppose that simple labour is itself taken as a measure of value? If the mere quantity of labour functions as a measure of value regardless of quality, it presupposes that simple labour has become the pivot of industry. It presupposes that labour has been equalized by the subordination of man to the machine or by the extreme division of labour; that men are effaced by their labour; that the pendulum of the clock has become as accurate a measure of the relative activity of two workers as it is of speed of two locomotives. Therefore, we should not say that one man's hour is worth another man's hour, but rather that one man during an hour is worth just as much as another man during an hour. Time is everything, man is nothing; he is at the most, time's carcase. Quality no longer matters. Quantity alone decides everything; hour for hour, day for day; but this equalizing of labour is not by any means the work of M. Proudhon's eternal justice; it is purely and simply a fact of modern industry.

P.P., pp. 53–54

But to consider matters more broadly: You would be altogether mistaken in fancying that the value of labour or any other commodity whatever is ultimately fixed by supply and demand. Supply and demand regulate nothing but the temporary *fluctuations* of market prices. They will explain to you why the market price of a commodity rises above or sinks below its *value*, but they can never account for that *value* itself. Suppose supply and demand to equilibrate, or, as the economists call it, to cover each other. Why, the very moment these opposite forces become equal they paralyse each other, and cease to work in the one or the other direction. At the moment when supply and demand equilibrate each other, and therefore cease to act, the *market* price of a commodity coincides with its *real value*, with the standard price round which its market prices oscillate. In inquiring into the nature of that *value*, we have, therefore, nothing at all to do with the temporary effects on market prices of supply and demand. The same holds true of wages and of the prices of all other commodities.

Wages, Price and Profit. S.W.I., pp. 413–14

. . . Taking one single commodity, wheat, for instance, we shall find that a quarter of wheat exchanges in almost countless variations of proportion with different commodities. Yet, *its value remaining always the same*, whether expressed in silk, gold, or any other commodity, it must be something distinct from, and independent of, these different *rates of exchange* with different articles. It must be possible to express, in a very different form, these various equations with various commodities.

Besides, if I say a quarter of wheat exchanges with iron in a certain proportion, or the value of a quarter of wheat is expressed in a certain amount of iron, I say that the value of wheat and its equivalent in iron are equal *to some third thing*, which is neither wheat nor iron, because I suppose them to express the same magnitude in two different shapes. Either of them, the wheat or the iron, must, therefore, independently of the other, be reducible to this third thing which is their common measure.

Wages, Price and Profit.   S.W.I., p. 417

If we consider *commodities as values*, we consider them exclusively under the single aspect of *realised, fixed*, or, if you like, *crystallised social labour*. In this respect they can *differ* only by representing greater or smaller quantities of labour, as, for example, a greater amount of labour may be worked up in a silken handkerchief than in a brick. But how does one measure *quantities of labour*? By the *time the labour lasts*, in measuring the labour by the hour, the day, etc. Of course, to apply this measure, all sorts of labour are reduced to average or simple labour as their unit.

We arrive, therefore, at this conclusion. A commodity has a *value*, because it is a *crystallisation of social labour*. The *greatness* of its value, of its *relative* value, depends upon the greater or less amount of that social substance contained in it; that is to say, on the relative mass of labour necessary for its production. The *relative values of commodities* are, therefore, determined by the *respective quantities or amounts of labour, worked up, realised, fixed in them*. The *correlative* quantities of commodities which can be produced in the *same time of labour* are *equal*. Or the value of one commodity is to the value of another commodity as the quantity of labour fixed in the one is to the quantity of labour fixed in the other.

Wages, Price and Profit.   S.W.I., p. 418

The value of a commodity would therefore remain constant, if the labour-time required for its production also remained constant. But the latter changes with every variation in the productiveness of labour. This productiveness is determined by various circumstances, amongst others, by the average amount of skill of the workmen, the state of science, and the degree of its practical application, the social organisation of production, the extent and capabilities of the means of production, and by physical conditions. For example, the same amount of labour in favourable seasons is embodied in 8 bushels of corn, and in unfavourable, only in four. The same labour extracts from rich mines more metal than from poor mines. Diamonds are of very rare occurrence on the earth's surface, and hence their discovery costs, on an average, a great deal of labour-time. . . . In general, the greater the productiveness of labour, the less is the labour-time required for the production of an article, the less is the amount of labour crystallised in that article, and the less is its value; and *vice versa*, the less the productiveness of labour, the greater is the labour-time required for the production of an article, and the greater is its value. The value of a commodity, therefore, varies directly as the quantity, and inversely as the productiveness, of the labour incorporated in it.

C.I., p. 40

[Price is the monetary expression of value. But the value of a commodity need not coincide, according to Marx, with its current exchange value, or price. Prices may rise because values have risen (if the value of money has not also risen), or because the value of money has fallen relative to that of other commodities. Supply, demand and competition account for short-term fluctuations in market prices.

Marx denied that prices are directly determined by wages, which, by means of political action, could sometimes be raised above subsistence level. Low-priced commodities, he wrote, are often produced by high-priced labour. Marx argued that a general rise in wages ultimately reduces profits, while leaving prices unaffected.]

The conflict does not take place between utility and estimation; it takes place between the marketable value demanded by the supplier and the marketable value supplied by the demander. The exchange value of the product is each time the resultant of these contradictory appreciations.

In final analysis, supply and demand bring together production and consumption, but production and consumption based on individual exchanges.

The product supplied is not useful in itself. It is the consumer who determines its utility. And even when its quality of being useful is admitted, it does not exclusively represent utility. In the course of production, it has been exchanged for all the costs of production, such as raw materials, wages of workers, etc., all of which are marketable values. The product, therefore, represents, in the eyes of the producer, a sum total of marketable values. What he supplies is not only a useful object, but also and above all a marketable value.

As to demand, it will only be effective on condition that it has means of exchange at its disposal. These means are themselves products, marketable value.

In supply and demand, then, we find, on the one hand, a product which has cost marketable values, and the need to sell; on the other, means which have cost marketable values, and the desire to buy.

The consumer is no freer than the producer. His judgment depends on his means and his needs. Both of these are determined by his social position, which itself depends on the whole social organisation. True, the worker who buys potatoes and the kept woman who buys lace both follow their respective judgments. But the difference in their judgments is explained by the difference in the positions which they occupy in the world, and which themselves are the product of social organisation.

Is the entire system of needs founded on estimation or on the whole organisation of production? Most often, needs arise directly from production or from a state of affairs based on production. World trade turns almost entirely round the needs, not of individual consumption, but of production. Thus, to choose another example, does not the need for lawyers suppose a given civil law which is but the expression of a certain development of property, that is to say, of production?

It is not enough for M. Proudhon to have eliminated the elements just mentioned from the relation of supply and demand. He carries abstraction to the furthest limits when he fuses all producers into *one single* producer, all consumers into *one single* consumer, and sets up a struggle between these two chimerical personages. But in the real world, things happen otherwise. The competition among the suppliers and the competition among the demanders form a necessary part of the struggle between buyers and sellers, of which marketable value is the result.

P.P., pp. 40–42

In calculating the exchangeable value of a commodity we must add to the quantity of labour *last* employed the quantity of labour *previously* worked up in the raw material of the commodity, and the labour bestowed on the implements, tools, machinery, and buildings, with which such labour is assisted. For example, the value of a certain amount of cotton-yarn is the crystallisation of the quantity of labour added to the cotton during the spinning process, the quantity of labour previously realised in the cotton itself, the quantity of labour realised in the coal, oil, and other auxiliary substances used, the quantity of labour fixed in the steam engine, the spindles, the factory buildings, and so forth. Instruments of production, properly so-called, such as tools, machinery, buildings, serve again and again for a longer or shorter period during repeated processes of production. If they were used up at once, like the raw material, their whole value would at once be transferred to the commodities they assist in producing. But as a spindle, for example, is but gradually used up, an average calculation is made, based upon the average time it lasts, and its average waste of wear and tear during a certain period, say a day. In this way we calculate how much of the value of the spindle is transferred to the yarn daily spun, and how much, therefore, of the total amount of labour realized in a pound of yarn, for example, is due to the quantity of labour previously realised in the spindle. For our present purpose it is not necessary to dwell any longer upon this point.

It might seem that if the value of a commodity is determined by the *quantity of labour bestowed upon its production*, the lazier a man, or the clumsier a man, the more valuable his commodity, because the greater the time of labour required for finishing the commodity. This, however, would be a sad mistake. You will recollect that I used the word '*Social* labour,' and many points are involved in this qualification of '*Social*'. In saying that the value of a commodity is determined by the *quantity o, labour* worked up or crystallised in it, we mean the *quantity of labour necessary* for its production in a given state of society, under certain social average conditions of production, with a given social average intensity, and average skill of the labour employed. When, in England, the power-loom came to compete with the hand-loom, only one half of the former time of labour was wanted to convert a given amount of yarn into a yard of cotton or cloth. The poor hand-loom weaver now worked seventeen or eighteen hours daily, instead of the nine or ten he had worked before. Still the product of twenty hours of his labour represented now only ten social hours of labour, or ten hours of labour socially necessary for the conversion of a certain amount of yarn into textile stuffs. His product of twenty hours had, therefore, no more value than his former product of ten hours.

If then the quantity of socially necessary labour realised in commodities regulates their exchangeable values, every increase in the quantity of labour wanted for the production of a commodity must augment its value, as every diminution must lower it.

Apart from the different natural energies and acquired working abilities of different peoples, the productive powers of labour must principally depend:

Firstly. Upon the *natural* conditions of labour, such as fertility of soil, mines, and so forth;

Secondly. Upon the progressive improvement of the *Social Powers of Labour*, such as are derived from production on a grand scale, concentration of capital and combination of labour, subdivision of labour, machinery, improved methods, appliance of chemical and other natural agencies, shortening of time and space by means of communication and transport, and every other contrivance by which science presses natural agencies into the service of labour, and by which the social or co-operative character of labour is developed. The greater the productive powers of labour, the less labour is bestowed upon a given amount of produce; hence the smaller the value of this produce. The smaller the productive powers of labour, the more labour is bestowed upon the same amount of produce; hence the greater its value. As a general law we may, therefore, set it down that:

The values of commodities are directly as the times of labour employed in their production, and are inversely as the productive powers of the labour employed.

Having till now only spoken of *Value*, I shall add a few words about *Price*, which is a peculiar form assumed by value.

Price, taken by itself, is nothing but the *monetary expression of value*. The values of all commodities in this country, for example, are expressed in gold prices, while on the Continent they are mainly expressed in silver prices. The value of gold or silver, like that of all other commodities, is regulated by the quantity of labour necessary for getting them. You exchange a certain amount of your national products, in which a certain amount of your national labour is crystallised, for the produce of the gold and silver producing countries, in which a certain quantity of *their* labour is crystallised. It is in this way, in fact by barter, that you learn to express in gold and silver the values of all commodities, that is, the respective quantities of labour bestowed upon them. Looking somewhat closer into the *monetary expression of value*, or what comes to the same, the conversion of value into price, you will find that it is a process by which you give to the *values* of all commodities an *independent* and *homogeneous form*, or by which you express them as quantities of equal social labour. So far as it is but the monetary expression of value, price has been called *natural price* by Adam Smith, *'prix nécessaire'* by the French physiocrats.

What then is the relation between *value* and *market prices*, or between *natural prices* and *market prices*? You all know that the *market* price is the *same* for all commodities of the same kind, however the conditions of production may differ for the individual producers. The market price expresses only the *average amount of social labour* necessary, under the average conditions of production, to supply the market with a certain mass of a certain article. It is calculated upon the whole lot of a commodity of a certain description.

So far the *market price* of a commodity coincides with its *value*. On the other hand, the oscillations of market prices, rising now over, sinking now under the value or natural price, depend upon the fluctuations of supply and demand. The deviations of market prices from values are continual, but as Adam Smith says: 'The natural price . . . is the central price, to which the prices of all commodities are continually gravitating. Different accidents may sometimes keep them suspended a good deal above it, and sometimes force them down even somewhat below it. But whatever may be the obstacles which hinder them from settling in this centre of repose and continuance they are constantly tending towards it.'

Wages, Price and Profit. S.W.I., pp. 419–23

[Marx held that profits and wages operate in inverse ratio to one another (a theory much more cheering to the working class than one which correlated wages with prices). A rise in wages, he said, leads to an increased demand on behalf of the workers for the necessities of life, which in turn compensates the capitalists in certain sectors for the rise in wages. Capital then migrates to those sectors until the supply and demand for capital are again in equilibrium throughout the economy. This leads finally to a general fall in profits without permanently affecting prices. A falling rate of profit is one of the symptoms of decaying capitalism.]

What, then, is the general law which determines the rise and fall of wages and profit in their reciprocal relation?

They stand in inverse ratio to each other. Capital's share, profit, rises in the same proportion as labour's share, wages, falls, and vice versa. Profit rises to the extent that wages fall; it falls to the extent that wages rise.

Wage Labour and Capital. S.W.I., p. 96

To explain, therefore, the *general nature of profits*, you must start from the theorem that, on an average, commodities are *sold at their real value*, and *that profits are derived from selling them at their values*, that is, in proportion to the quantity of labour realised in them. If you cannot explain profit upon this supposition, you cannot explain it at all. This seems paradox and contrary to everyday observation. It is also paradox that the earth moves round the sun, and that water consists of two highly inflammable gases. Scientific truth is always paradox, if judged by everyday experience, which catches only the delusive appearance of things.

Wages, Price and Profit. S.W.I., p. 424

The *surplus value*, or that part of the total value of the commodity in which the *surplus labour* or *unpaid labour* of the working man is realised, I call *Profit*. The whole of that profit is not pocketed by the employing capitalist. The monopoly of land enables the landlord to take one part of that *surplus value*, under the name of *rent*, whether the land is used for agriculture, buildings or railways, or for any other productive purpose. On the other hand, the very fact that the possession of the *instruments of labour* enables the employing capitalist to produce a *surplus value*, or, what comes to the same, to *appropriate to himself a certain amount of unpaid labour*, enables the owner of the means of labour, which he lends wholly or partly to the employing capitalist – enables, in one word, the money-lending capitalist to claim for himself under the name of *interest* another part of that surplus value, so that there remains to the employing capitalist *as such* only what is called *industrial* or *commercial profit*.

Rent, Interest, and Industrial Profit are only *different names for different parts of* the *surplus value* of the commodity, or the *unpaid labour enclosed in it*, and they *are equally derived from this source, and from this source alone*. They are not derived from *land* as such or from *capital* as such, but land and capital enable their owners to get their respective shares out of the surplus value extracted by the employing capitalist from the labourer. . . .

Wages, Price and Profit.   S.W.I., p. 431

Then again, a general rise in wages can never produce a more or less general rise in the price of goods. Actually, if every industry employed the same number of workers in relation to fixed capital or to the instruments used, a general rise in wages would produce a general fall in profits and the current price of goods would undergo no alteration.

But as the relation of manual labour to fixed capital is not the same in different industries, all the industries which employ a relatively greater mass of capital and fewer workers, will be forced sooner or later to lower the price of their goods. In the opposite case, in which the price of their goods is not lowered, their profit will rise above the common rate of profits. Machines are not wage-earners. Therefore, the general rise in wages will affect less those industries, which, compared with the others, employ more machines than workers. But as competition always tends to level the rate of profits, those profits which rise above the average rate cannot but be transitory. Thus, apart from a few fluctuations, a general rise in wages will lead, not as M. Proudhon says, to a general increase in prices, but to a partial fall, that is a fall in the current price of the goods that are made chiefly with the help of machines.

The rise and fall of profits and wages expresses merely the proportion in which capitalists and workers share in the product of a day's work, without influencing in most instances the price of the product. But that 'strikes followed by an increase in wages culminate in a general rise in prices, in a dearth even' – these are notions which can blossom only in the brain of a poet who has not been understood.

P.P., p. 167

E. The Future of Capitalism

[In the passage which follows, the nature and extent of Marx's
ethical and emotional rejection of capitalist society stands out
clearly. The relation of ethics to dialectical materialism is of
course a contentious and delicate one. But Marx was by no
means the first to catalogue the evils of capitalism. Engels had
done so in 1844, and Marx had made notes on the works of
John Bray, Thomas Cooper, T. R. Edmonds, Robert Owen,
Andrew Ure and Thomas Hodgskin.]

M. Proudhon talks of nothing but modern monopoly engendered by competition. But we all know that competition
was engendered by feudal monopoly. Thus competition was
originally the opposite of monopoly and not monopoly the
opposite of competition. So that modern monopoly is not a
simple antithesis, it is on the contrary the true synthesis.

Thesis: Feudal monopoly, before competition.

Antithesis: Competition.

Synthesis: Modern monopoly, which is the negation of feudal
monopoly, in so far as it implies the system of competition, and
the negation of competition in so far as it is monopoly.

Thus modern monopoly, bourgeois monopoly, is synthetic
monopoly, the negation of the negation, the unity of opposites.
It is monopoly in the pure, normal, rational state.

P.P., p. 151

In practical life we find not only competition, monopoly and
the antagonism between them, but also the synthesis of the
two, which is not a formula, but a movement. Monopoly
produces competition, competition produces monopoly. Monopolists are made from competition; competitors become

monopolists. If the monopolists restrict their mutual competition by means of partial associations, competition increases among the workers; and the more the mass of the proletarians grows as against the monopolists of one nation, the more desperate competition becomes between the monopolists of different nations. The synthesis is of such a character that monopoly can only maintain itself by continually entering into the struggle of competition.

P.P., p. 152

In the same way, feudal landed property gives its name to its lord, as does a kingdom to its king. His family history, the history of his house, etc. – all this individualises the estate for him and makes it literally his house, personifies it. Similarly those working on the estate have not the position of *day-labourers*; but they are in part themselves his property, as are serfs; and in part they are bound to him by ties of respect, allegiance and duty. His relation to them is therefore directly political, and has likewise a human, *intimate* side. Customs, character, etc., vary from one estate to another and seem to be one with the land to which they belong; later, on the other hand, a man is bound to his land, not by his character or his individuality, but only by his purse strings. Finally, the feudal lord does not try to extract the utmost advantage from his land. Rather, he consumes what is there and calmly leaves the worry of producing to the serfs and the tenants. Such is *nobility's* relationship to landed property, which casts a romantic glory on its lords.

It is necessary that this appearance be abolished – that landed property, the root of private property, be dragged completely into the movement of private property and that it become a commodity; that the rule of the proprietor appear as the undisguised rule of private property, of capital, freed of all political tincture; that the relationship between proprietor and worker be reduced to the economic relationship of exploiter and exploited; that all personal relationship between the proprietor and his property cease, property becoming merely *objective*, material wealth; that the marriage of convenience should take the place of the marriage of honour with the land; and that the land should likewise sink to the status of a commercial value, like man. It is essential that that which is the root of landed property – filthy self-interest – make its appearance, too, in its cynical form. It is essential that the immovable monopoly turn into the mobile and restless monopoly, into competition; and that the idle enjoyment of the products of the other peoples' blood and toil turn into a bustling commerce in the same commodity. Lastly, it is essential that in this competition landed property, in the form of capital, manifest its dominion over both the working class and the proprietors themselves who are either being ruined or raised by the laws governing the movement of capital. The medieval proverb *nulle terre sans seigneur* is thereby replaced by that other proverb, *l'argent n'a pas de maître* wherein is expressed the complete domination of dead matter over men. E.P.M., pp. 62–63

. . . The point of bourgeois society consists precisely in this, that *a priori* there is no conscious, social regulation of production. The rational and naturally necessary asserts itself only as a blindly working average. . . .

Marx to L. Kugelmann, July 11, 1868. S.W.II., p. 462

Mr. Broughton Charlton, county magistrate, declared, as chairman of a meeting held at the Assembly Rooms, Nottingham, on January 14, 1860, 'that there was an amount of privation and suffering among that portion of the population connected with the lace trade, unknown in other parts of the kingdom, indeed, in the civilised world . . . Children of nine or ten years are dragged from their squalid beds at two, three, or four o'clock in the morning and compelled to work for a bare subsistence until ten, eleven, or twelve at night, their limbs wearing away, their frames dwindling, their faces whitening, and their humanity absolutely sinking into a stone-like torpor, utterly horrible to contemplate . . . We are not surprised that Mr. Mallett, or any other manufacturer, should stand forward

and protest against discussion. . . . The system, as the Rev.
Montagu Valpy describes it, is one of unmitigated slavery,
socially, physically, morally, and spiritually. . . . What can be
thought of a town which holds a public meeting to petition
that the period of labour for men shall be diminished to eighteen
hours a day? . . . We declaim against the Virginian and Caro-
linian cotton-planters. Is their black-market, their lash, and
their barter of human flesh more detestable than the slow
sacrifice of humanity which takes place in order that veils and
collars may be fabricated for the benefit of capitalists?'

C.I., pp. 243–4

From the report of the Commissioners in 1863, the following:
Dr. J. T. Arledge, senior physician of the North Staffordshire
Infirmary, says: 'The potters as a class, both men and women,
represent a degenerated population, both physically and morally.
They are, as a rule, stunted in growth, ill-shaped, and frequently
ill-formed in the chest; they become prematurely old, and are
certainly short-lived; they are phlegmatic and bloodless, and
exhibit their debility of constitution by obstinate attacks of
dyspepsia, and disorders of the liver and kidneys, and by
rheumatism. But of all diseases they are especially prone to
chest-disease, to pneumonia, phthisis, bronchitis, and asthma.
One form would appear peculiar to them, and is known as
potter's asthma, or potter's consumption Scrofula attacking the
glands, or bones, or other parts of the body, is a disease of
two-thirds or more of the potters. . . . That the "degeneres-
cence" of the population of this district is not even greater than
it is, is due to the constant recruiting from the adjacent country,
and intermarriages with more healthy races.'   C.I., p. 245

. . . The decisively revolutionary machine, the machine which
attacks in an equal degree the whole of the numberless branches
of this sphere of production, dressmaking, tailoring, shoemaking,
sewing, hat-making, and many others, is the sewing-machine.

Its immediate effect on the workpeople is like that of all
machinery, which, since the rise of modern industry, has seized
upon new branches of trade. Children of too tender an age are

sent adrift. The wage of the machine hands rises compared with that of the house-workers, many of whom belong to the poorest of the poor. That of the better situated handicraftsmen, with whom the machine competes, sinks. The new machine hands are exclusively girls and young women. With the help of mechanical force, they destroy the monopoly that male labour had of the heavier work, and they drive off from the lighter work numbers of old women and very young children. The overpowering competition crushes the weakest of the manual labourers. The fearful increase in death from starvation during the last 10 years in London runs parallel with the extension of machine sewing. The new workwomen turn the machines by hand and foot, or by hand alone, sometimes sitting, sometimes standing, according to the weight, size, and special make of the machine, and expend a great deal of labour-power. Their occupation is unwholesome, owing to the long hours, although in most cases they are not so long as under the old system. Wherever the sewing-machine locates itself in narrow and already over-crowded workrooms, it adds to the unwholesome influences. 'The effect,' says Mr. Lord, 'on entering low-ceiled workrooms in which 30 to 40 machine hands are working is unbearable . . . The heat, partly due to the gas stoves used for warming the irons, is horrible . . . Even when moderate hours of work, i.e. from 8 in the morning till 6 in the evening, prevail in such places, yet 3 or 4 persons fall into a swoon regularly every day.'   C.I., pp. 471–2

Newcastle-on-Tyne, as the centre of a coal and iron district of growing productiveness, takes the next place after London in the housing inferno. Not less than 34,000 persons live there in single rooms. Because of their absolute danger to the community, houses in great number have lately been destroyed by the authorities in Newcastle and Gateshead. The building of new houses progresses very slowly, business very quickly. The town was, therefore, in 1865, more full than ever. Scarcely a room was to let. Dr. Embleton, of the Newcastle Fever Hospital, says: 'There can be little doubt that the great cause of the continuance and spread of the typhus has been the over-crowding of human beings, and the uncleanliness of their dwellings. The rooms, in which labourers in many cases live, are situated in confined and unwholesome yards or courts, and for space, light, air, and cleanliness, are models of insufficiency and insalubrity, and a disgrace to any civilised community; in them men, women, and children lie at night huddled together; and as regards the men, the night-shift succeeds the day-shift, and the day-shift the night-shift in unbroken series for some time together, the beds having scarcely time to cool; the whole house badly supplied with water and worse with privies; dirty, unventilated, and pestiferous.' The price per week of such lodgings ranges from 8d. to 3s. 'The town of Newcastle-on-Tyne,' says Dr. Hunter, 'contains a sample of the finest tribe of our countrymen, often sunk by external circumstances of house and street into an almost savage degradation.'

C.I., p. 661

[Marx's important thesis about the tendency of capitalism progressively to pauperise the proletariat has been interpreted in more ways than one. Obviously Marx regarded the swelling of the ranks of the working class and its continual degradation as the pre-requisites of revolution. But did he imply absolute impoverishment or merely relative impoverishment – relative to the standard of living enjoyed by other classes? Passages from Marx can be found to support either view. Certainly the real wages of the English workers rose sharply in the two decades after 1848, a fact which he acknowledged. It was paradoxical, perhaps, that Marx constantly urged the British workers to fight for higher wages and a shorter working day, while at the same time teaching that the reforming struggle was ultimately a hopeless one.]

(c) In an increasingly prosperous society it is only the very richest people who can go on living on money-interest. Everyone else has to carry on a business with his capital, or venture it in trade. As a result, the competition between capitals becomes more intense. The concentration of capitals increases, the big capitalists ruin the small, and a section of the erstwhile capitalists sinks into the working class, which as a result of this supply again suffers to some extent a depression of wages and passes into a still greater dependence on the few big capitalists. The number of capitalists having been diminished, their competition with respect to workers scarcely exists any longer; and the number of workers having been augmented, their competition among themselves has become all the more intense, unnatural and violent. Consequently, a section of the working class falls into the ranks of beggary or starvation just as necessarily as a section of the middle capitalists falls into the working class.

E.P.M., pp. 24–25

The lower strata of the middle class – the small tradespeople, shopkeepers, and retired tradesmen generally, the handicrafts-men and peasants – all these sink gradually into the proletariat, partly because their diminutive capital does not suffice for the scale on which Modern Industry is carried on, and is swamped in the competition with the large capitalists, partly because their specialised skill is rendered worthless by new methods of production. Thus the proletariat is recruited from all classes of the population.

C.M., pp. 59–60

The real facts, which are travestied by the optimism of econo-mists, are as follows: The labourers, when driven out of the workshop by the machinery, are thrown upon the labour-market, and there add to the number of workmen at the disposal of the capitalists. In Part VII of this book it will be seen that this effect of machinery, which, as we have seen, is represented to be a compensation to the working-class, is on the contrary, a most frightful scourge. For the present I will only say this: The labourers that are thrown out of work in any branch of industry, can no doubt seek for employment in some other branch. If they find it, and thus renew the bond between them and the means of subsistence, this takes place only by the intermediary of a new and additional capital that is seeking investment; not at all by the intermediary of the capital that formerly employed them and was afterwards converted into machinery. And even should they find employment, what a poor look-out is theirs! Crippled as they are by division of labour, these poor devils are worth so little outside their old trade, that they cannot find admission into any industries, except a few of inferior kind, that are over-supplied with underpaid workmen. Further, every branch of industry attracts each year a new stream of men, who furnish a contingent from which to fill up vacancies, and to draw a supply for expansion. So soon as machinery sets free a part of the workmen employed in a given branch of industry, the reserve men are also diverted into new channels of employment, and become absorbed in other branches; meanwhile the original victims, during the period of transition, for the most part starve and perish.

C.I., pp. 440–1

. . . Indeed, with local colours changed, and on a scale some-what contracted, the English facts reproduce themselves in all the industrious and progressive countries of the Continent. In all of them there has taken place, since 1848, an unheard-of de-velopment of industry, and an undreamed-of expansion of imports and exports. In all of them 'the augmentation of wealth and power entirely confined to classes of property' was truly 'intoxicating'. In all of them, as in England, a minority of the working classes got their real wages somewhat advanced; while in most cases the monetary rise of wages denoted no more a real access of comforts than the inmate of the metropolitan poor-house or orphan asylum, for instance, was in the least benefited by his first necessaries costing £9 15s. 8d. in 1861 against £7 7s. 4d. in 1852. Everywhere the great mass of the working classes were sinking down to a lower depth, at the same rate at least, that those above them were rising in the social scale. In all countries of Europe it has now become a truth demonstrable to every unprejudiced mind, and only denied by those, whose interest it is to hedge other people in a fool's paradise, that no improvement of machinery, no appliance of science to production, no contrivances of communication, no new colonies, no emigration, no opening of markets, no free trade, nor all these things put together, will do away with the miseries of the industrious masses; but that, on the present false base, every fresh development of the productive powers of labour must tend to deepen social contrasts and point social antagonisms. Death of starvation rose almost to the rank of an institution, during this intoxicating epoch of economical progress, in the metropolis of the British Empire. That epoch is marked in the annals of the world by the quickened return, the widening compass, and the deadlier effects of the social pest called a commercial and industrial crisis.

Inaugural Address of the Working
Men's International Association, 1864.   S.W.I., p. 381

[Marx was adamant that capitalism could neither reform nor rescue itself. The passage which follows, and Engels' later explanation in the footnote, indicates Marx's tendency towards dogmatism. Later, in 1875, he remarked that a general prohibition of child-labour under capitalism was an impossibility.]

Direct slavery is just as much the pivot of bourgeois industry as machinery, credits, etc. Without slavery you have no cotton; without cotton you have no modern industry. It is slavery that gave the colonies their value; it is the colonies that created world trade, and it is world trade that is the pre-condition of large-scale industry. Thus slavery is an economic category of the greatest importance.

Without slavery, North America, the most progressive of countries, would be transformed into a patriarchal country. Wipe North America off the map of the world, and you will have anarchy – the complete decay of modern commerce and civilisation. Cause slavery to disappear and you will have wiped America off the map of nations.*   P.P., pp. 111–12

[Capitalism is doomed by its own inherent laws, teaches Marx. The principal factors in the process of self-destruction are as follows: (a) worsening economic crises, the expansion of the market having failed to keep pace with the expansion of production; (b) a falling rate of profit; (c) the destruction of the middle classes and the formation of a vast, increasingly depressed proletariat; (d) the tendency towards monopoly within capitalism prepares the mode of production for socialism.   ]

The *real barrier* of capitalist production is *capital itself*. It is that capital and its self-expansion appear as the starting and the closing point, the motive and the purpose of production; that production is only production for *capital* and not vice versa, the means of production are not mere means for a constant expansion of the living process of the *society* or producers. The limits within which the preservation and self-expansion of the value of capital resting on the expropriation and pauperisation of the great mass of producers can alone move – these limits come continually into conflict with the methods of production employed by capital for its purpose, which drive towards unlimited extension of production, towards production as an end in itself, towards unconditional development of the social productivity of labour. The means – unconditional development of the productive forces of society – comes continually into conflict with the limited purpose, the self-expansion of the

---

* This was perfectly correct for the year 1847. At that time the world trade of the United States was limited mainly to import of immigrants and industrial products, and export of cotton and tobacco, i.e. of the products of southern slave labour. The Northern States produced mainly corn and meat for the slave states. It was only when the North produced corn and meat for export and also became an industrial country, and when the American cotton monopoly had to face powerful competition, in India, Egypt, Brazil, etc., that the abolition of slavery became possible. And even then this led to the ruin of the South, which did not succeed in replacing the open Negro slavery by the disguised slavery of Indian and Chinese coolies. [*Note by F. Engels to the German edition, 1885.*]

existing capital. The capitalist mode of production is, for this reason, a historical means of developing the material forces of production and creating an appropriate world-market and is, at the same time, a continual conflict between this its historical task and its own corresponding relations of social production.

C.III., p. 245

As soon as this process of transformation has sufficiently decomposed the old society from top to bottom, as soon as the labourers are turned into proletarians, their means of labour into capital, as soon as the capitalist mode of production stands on its own feet, then the further socialisation of labour and further transformation of the land and other means of production into socially exploited, and, therefore, common means of production, as well as the further expropriation of private proprietors, takes a new form. That which is now to be expropriated is no longer the labourer working for himself, but the capitalist exploiting many labourers. This expropriation is accomplished by the action of the immanent laws of capitalistic production itself, by the centralisation of capital. One capitalist always kills many. Hand in hand with this centralisation, or this expropriation of many capitalists by few, develop, on an ever-extending scale, the co-operative form of the labour-process, the conscious technical application of science, the methodical cultivation of the soil, the transformation of the instruments of labour into instruments of labour only usable in common, the economising of all means of production by their use as the means of production of combined, socialised labour, the entanglement of all peoples in the net of the world-market, and with this, the international character of the capitalistic régime. Along with the constantly diminishing number of the magnates of capital, who usurp and monopolise all advantages of this process of transformation, grows the mass of misery, oppression, slavery, degradation, exploitation; but with this too grows the revolt of the working-class, a class always increasing in numbers, and disciplined, united, organised by the very mechanism of the process of capitalist production itself. The monopoly of capital becomes a fetter upon the mode of production, which has sprung up and flourished along with, and under it. Centralisation of the means of production and socialisation of labour at last reach a point where they become incompatible with their capitalist integument. This integument is burst asunder. The knell of capitalist private property sounds. The expropriators are expropriated.

The capitalist mode of appropriation, the result of the capitalist mode of production, produces capitalist private property. This is the first negation of individual private property, as founded on the labour of the proprietor. But capitalist production begets, with the inexorability of a law of Nature, its own negation. It is the negation of negation. This does not re-establish private property for the producer, but gives him individual property based on the acquisitions of the capitalist era: i.e. on co-operation and the possession in common of the land and of the means of production.

The transformation of scattered private property, arising from individual labour, into capitalist private property, is, naturally, a process, incomparably more protracted, violent, and difficult, than the transformation of capitalistic private property, already practically resting on socialised production, into socialised property. In the former case, we had the expropriation of the mass of the people by a few usurpers; in the latter, we have the expropriation of a few usurpers by the mass of the people.

C.I., pp. 762–4

There are not too many necessities of life produced, in proportion to the existing population. Quite the reverse. Too little is produced to decently and humanely satisfy the wants of the great mass.

There are not too many means of production produced to employ the able-bodied portion of the population. Quite the reverse. In the first place, too large a portion of the produced population is not really capable of working, and is through force of circumstances made dependent on exploiting the labour of others, or on labour which can pass under this name only under a miserable mode of production. In the second place, not enough means of production are produced to permit the employment of the entire able-bodied population under the most productive conditions, so that their absolute working period could be shortened by the mass and effectiveness of the constant capital employed during working-hours.

On the other hand, too many means of labour and necessities of life are produced at times to permit of their serving as means for the exploitation of labourers at a certain rate of profit. Too many commodities are produced to permit of a realisation and conversion into new capital of the value and surplus-value contained in them under the conditions of distribution and consumption peculiar to capitalist production, i.e. too many to permit of the consummation of this process without constantly recurring explosions.

Not too much wealth is produced. But at times too much wealth is produced in its capitalistic, self-contradictory forms.

The limitations of the capitalist mode of production come to the surface:

(1) In that the development of the productivity of labour creates out of the falling rate of profit a law which at a certain point comes into antagonistic conflict with this development and must be overcome constantly through crises.

(2) In that the expansion or contraction of production are determined by the appropriation of unpaid labour and the proportion of this unpaid labour to materialised labour in general, or, to speak the language of the capitalists, by profit and the proportion of this profit to the employed capital, thus by a definite rate of profit, rather than the relation of production to social requirements, i.e. to the requirements of socially developed human beings. It is for this reason that the capitalist mode of production meets with barriers at a certain expanded stage of production which, if viewed from the other premise, would reversely have been altogether inadequate. It comes to a standstill at a point fixed by the production and realisation of profit, and not the satisfaction of requirements.

C.III., pp. 252–3

The essential condition for the existence, and for the sway of the bourgeois class, is the formation and augmentation of capital; the condition for capital is wage labour. Wage labour rests exclusively on competition between the labourers. The

advance of industry, whose involuntary promoter is the bourgeoisie, replaces the isolation of the labourers, due to competition,
by their revolutionary combination, due to association. The
development of Modern Industry, therefore, cuts from under
its feet the very foundation on which the bourgeoisie produces
and appropriates products. What the bourgeoisie, therefore,
produces, above all, is its own gravediggers. Its fall and the
victory of the proletariat are equally inevitable.

C.M., pp. 67–68

... It is enough to mention the commercial crises that by their
periodical return put on its trial, each time more threateningly,
the existence of the entire bourgeois society. In these crises a
great part not only of the existing products, but also of the
previously created productive forces, are periodically destroyed.
In these crises there breaks out an epidemic that, in all earlier
epochs, would have seemed an absurdity – the epidemic of
over-production. Society suddenly finds itself put back into a
state of momentary barbarism; it appears as if a famine, a
universal war of devastation had cut off the supply of every
means of subsistence; industry and commerce seem to be
destroyed; and why? Because there is too much civilisation,
too much means of subsistence, too much industry, too much
commerce. The productive forces at the disposal of society no
longer tend to further the development of the conditions of
bourgeois property; on the contrary, they have become too
powerful for these conditions, by which they are fettered, and
so soon as they overcome these fetters, they bring disorder into
the whole of bourgeois society, endanger the existence of
bourgeois property. The conditions of bourgeois society are
too narrow to comprise the wealth created by them. And
how does the bourgeoisie get over these crises? On the one
hand by enforced destruction of a mass of productive forces;
on the other, by the conquest of new markets, and by the more
thorough exploitation of the old ones. That is to say, by paving
the way for more extensive and more destructive crises, and by
diminishing the means whereby crises are prevented.

The weapons with which the bourgeoisie felled feudalism to the ground are now turned against the bourgeoisie itself.

But not only has the bourgeoisie forged the weapons that bring death to itself; it has also called into existence the men who are to wield those weapons – the modern working class – the proletarians

C.M., pp. 55–57

PART FOUR

The Revolutionary Movement

A. The State

[The overthrow of capitalism entailed the overthrow of the
capitalist state, and its replacement by one dominated by the
proletariat. But what, in Marx's view, is the state?

For Hegel, man achieves ultimate reintegration with the
world in the perfected state. The Young Hegelians of the Left
regarded the contemporary Prussian state as the very opposite
of perfection. But they remained optimistic about the possibilities
of perfecting the state, and Marx to some extent shared this
optimism, at least until 1843. Thereafter he regarded the state
as such – any state – as the negation of man.

The state, like religion and money, he now described as a
manifestation of human alienation. Hence his paradoxical argu-
ment that the purely secular or democratic state is the one in
which the essentially religious character of states as such shows
through most clearly. It is the pure state.]

The Jewish question presents itself differently according to the
state in which the Jew resides. In Germany, where there is no
political state, no state as such, the Jewish question is purely
theological. The Jew finds himself in *religious* opposition to the
state, which proclaims Christianity as its foundation. This state
is a theologian *ex professo*. Criticism here is criticism of theology;
a double-edged criticism, of Christian and of Jewish theology.
And so we move always in the domain of theology, however
critically we may move therein.

In France, which is a *constitutional* state, the Jewish question
is a question of constitutionalism, of the incompleteness of
political emancipation. Since the *semblance* of a state religion is
maintained here, if only in the insignificant and self-contradictory
formula of a *religion of the majority*, the relation of the Jews to
the state also retains a semblance of religious, theological
opposition.

It is only in the free states of North America, or at least in some of them, that the Jewish question loses its *theological* significance and becomes a truly *secular* question. Only where the state exists in its completely developed form can the relation of the Jew, and of the religious man in general, to the political state appear in a pure form, with its own characteristics. The criticism of this relation ceases to be theological criticism when the state ceases to maintain a *theological* attitude towards religion, that is, when it adopts the attitude of a state, i.e. a *political* attitude. Criticism then becomes *criticism of the political state*. . . .

'Bruno Bauer, "Die Judenfrage".' E.W., pp. 8–9

Man emancipates himself *politically* from religion by expelling it from the sphere of public law to that of private law. Religion is no longer the spirit of the *state*, in which man behaves, albeit in a specific and limited way and in a particular sphere, as a species-being, in community with other men. It has become the spirit of *civil society*, of the sphere of egoism and of the *bellum omnium contra omnes*. It is no longer the essence of *community*, but the essence of *differentiation*. It has become what it was at the *beginning*, an expression of the fact that man is *separated* from the *community*, from himself and from other men. It is now only the abstract avowal of an individual folly, a private whim or caprice. The infinite fragmentation of religion in North America, for example, already gives it the *external* form of a strictly private affair. It has been relegated among the numerous private interests and exiled from the life of the community as such. But one should have no illusions about the scope of political emancipation. The division of man into the *public person* and the *private person*, the *displacement* of religion from the state to civil society – all this is not a stage in political emancipation but its consummation. Thus political emancipation does not abolish, and does not even strive to abolish, man's *real* religiosity.

In fact, the perfected Christian state is not the so-called *Christian* state which acknowledges Christianity as its basis, as the state religion, and thus adopts an exclusive attitude towards other religions; it is, rather, the *atheistic* state, the democratic state, the state which relegates religion among the other elements of civil society. The state which is still theological, which still professes officially the Christian creed, and which has not yet dared to declare itself a *state*, has not yet succeeded in expressing n a *human* and *secular* form, in its political *reality*, the human basis of which Christianity is the transcendental expression. The so-called Christian state is simply a *non-state*; since it is not Christianity as a religion, but only the *human core* of the Christian religion which can realise itself in truly human creations.

The so-called Christian state is the Christian negation of the state, but not at all the political realisation of Christianity. The state which professes Christianity as a religion does not yet profess it in a political form, because it still has a religious attitude towards religion. In other words, such a state is not the *genuine realisation* of the human basis of religion, because it still accepts the *unreal*, *imaginary* form of this human core. The so-called Christian state is an *imperfect* state, for which the Christian religion serves as the *supplement* and *sanctification* of its imperfection. Thus religion becomes necessarily one of its *means*; and so it is the *hypocritical* state. There is a great difference between saying: (i) that the *perfect* state, owing to a deficiency in the general *nature* of the state, counts religion as one of its *prerequisites*, or (ii) that the *imperfect* state, owing to a deficiency in its *particular existence* as an imperfect state, declares that religion is its *basis*. In the latter, religion becomes *imperfect politics*. In the former, the imperfection even of perfected *politics* is revealed in religion. The so-called Christian state needs the Christian religion in order to complete itself *as a state*. The democratic state, the real state, does not need religion for its political consummation. On the contrary, it can dispense with religion, because in this case the human core of religion is realised in a profane manner. The so-called Christian state, on the other hand, has a political attitude towards religion, and a religious attitude towards politics. It reduces political institutions and religion equally to mere appearances.

'Bruno Bauer, "Die Judenfrage".' E.W., pp. 15–17

But the religious spirit cannot be *really* secularised. For what is it but the *non-secular* form of a stage in the development of the human spirit? The religious spirit can only be realised if the stage of development of the human spirit which it expresses in religious form, manifests and constitutes itself in its *secular* form. This is what happens in the *democratic* state. The basis of this state is not Christianity but the *human basis* of Christianity. Religion remains the ideal, non-secular consciousness of its members, because it is the ideal form of the *stage of human development* which has been attained.

The members of the political state are religious because of the dualism between individual life and species-life, between the life of civil society and political life. They are religious in the sense that man treats political life, which is remote from his own individual existence, as if it were his true life; and in the sense that religion is here the spirit of civil society, and expresses the separation and withdrawal of man from man. Political democracy is Christian in the sense that man, not merely one man but every man, is there considered a sovereign being, a supreme being; but it is uneducated, unsocial man, man just as he is in his fortuitous existence, man as he has been corrupted, lost to himself, alienated, subjected to the rule of inhuman conditions and elements, by the whole organisation of our society – in short man who is not yet a *real* species-being. Creations of fantasy, dreams, the postulates of Christianity, the sovereignty of man – but of man as an alien being distinguished from the real man – all these become, in democracy, the tangible and present reality, secular maxims.

'Bruno Bauer, "Die Judenfrage".' E.W., p. 20

[In a striking passage Marx analyses in abstract terms the rise of the modern bourgeois state and its relation to civil society as manifestations of the progressive alienation of man.]

Political emancipation is at the same time the *dissolution* of the old society, upon which the sovereign power, the alienated political life of the people, rests. Political revolution is a revolution of civil society. What was the nature of the old society? It can be characterised in one word: *feudalism*. The old civil society had a *directly political* character; that is, the elements of civil life such as property, the family, and types of occupation had been raised, in the form of lordship, caste and guilds, to elements of political life. They determined, in this form, the relation of the individual to the *state as a whole*; that is, his *political* situation, or in other words, his separation and exclusion from the other elements of society. For this organisation of national life did not constitute property and labour as social elements; it rather succeeded in *separating* them from the body of the state, and made them *distinct* societies within society. Nevertheless, at least in the feudal sense, the vital functions and conditions of civil society remained political. They excluded the individual from the body of the state, and transformed the *particular* relation which existed between his corporation and the state into a general relation between the individual and social life, just as they transformed his specific civil activity and situation into a general activity and situation. As a result of this organisation, the state as a whole and its consciousness, will and activity – the general political power – also necessarily appeared as the *private* affair of a ruler and his servants, separated from the people.

The political revolution which overthrew this power of the ruler, which made state affairs the affairs of the people, and the political state a matter of *general* concern, i.e. a real state, necessarily shattered everything – estates, corporations, guilds, privileges – which expressed the separation of the people from community life. The political revolution therefore *abolished* the *political character of civil society*. It dissolved civil society into its basic elements, on the one hand *individuals*, and on the other hand, the *material and cultural elements* which formed the life experience and the civil situation of these individuals. It set free the political spirit which had, so to speak, been dissolved, fragmented and lost in the various cul-de-sac of feudal society; it reassembled these scattered fragments, liberated the political spirit from its connexion with civil life and made of it the community sphere, the *general* concern of the people, in principle independent of these particular elements of civil life. A *specific* activity and situation in life no longer had any but an individual significance. They no longer constituted the general relation between the individual and the state as a whole. Public affairs as such became the general affair of each individual, and political functions became general functions.

But the consummation of the idealism of the state was at the same time the consummation of the materialism of civil society. The bonds which had restrained the egoistic spirit of civil society were removed along with the political yoke. Political emancipation was at the same time an emancipation of civil society from politics and from even the *semblance* of a general content.

Feudal society was dissolved into its basic element, *man*; but into *egoistic* man who was its real foundation.

Man in this aspect, the member of civil society, is now the foundation and presupposition of the *political* state. He is recognised as such in the rights of man.

But the liberty of egoistic man, and the recognition of this liberty, is rather the recognition of the *frenzied* movement of the cultural and material elements which form the content of his life.

Thus man was not liberated from religion; he received religious liberty. He was not liberated from property; he received the liberty to own property. He was not liberated from the egoism of business; he received the liberty to engage in business.

The *formation of the political state*, and the dissolution of civil society into independent *individuals* whose relations are regulated by *law*, as the relations between men in the corporations and guilds were regulated by *privilege*, are accomplished by *one and the same act*. Man as a member of civil society – *non-political* man – necessarily appears as the *natural* man. The rights of man appear as natural rights because *conscious* activity is concentrated upon political *action*. *Egoistic* man is the passive, *given* result of the dissolution of society, an object of *direct apprehension* and consequently a *natural* object. The *political revolution* dissolves civil society into its elements without *revolutionising* these elements themselves or subjecting them to criticism. This revolution regards civil society, the sphere of human needs, labour, private interests and civil law, as the *basis of its own existence*, as a self-subsistent *precondition*, and thus as its *natural basis*. Finally, man as a member of civil society is identified with *authentic man*, *man* as distinct from citizen, because he is man in his sensuous, individual and *immediate* existence, whereas *political* man is only abstract, artificial man, man as an *allegorical*, *moral* person. Thus man as he really is, is seen only in the form of *egoistic* man, and man in his *true* nature only in the form of the *abstract citizen*.

The abstract notion of political man is well formulated by Rousseau: 'Whoever dares undertake to establish a people's institutions must feel himself capable of *changing*, as it were, *human nature* itself, of *transforming* each individual who, in isolation, is a complete but solitary whole, into a *part* of something greater than himself, from which in a sense, he derives his life and his being; [of changing man's nature in order to strengthen it]; of substituting a limited and moral existence for the physical and independent life [with which all of us are endowed by nature]. His task, in short, is to take from *a man his own powers*, and to give him in exchange alien powers which he can only employ with the help of other men.'

Every emancipation is a *restoration* of the human world and of human relationships to *man himself*.

Political emancipation is a reduction of man, on the one hand to a member of civil society, an *independent* and *egoistic* individual, and on the other hand, to a *citizen*, to a moral person.

Human emancipation will only be complete when the real, individual man has absorbed into himself the abstract citizen; when as an individual man, in his everyday life, in his work, and in his relationships, he has become a *species-being*; and when he has recognised and organised his own powers *(forces propres)* as *social* powers so that he no longer separates this social power from himself as *political* power.

'Bruno Bauer, "Die Judenfrage".' E.W., pp. 27–31

The perfected political state is, by its nature, the *species-life* of man as *opposed* to his material life. All the presuppositions of this egoistic life continue to exist in *civil society outside* the political sphere, as qualities of civil society. Where the political state has attained to its full development, man leads, not only in thought, in consciousness, but in *reality*, in *life*, a double existence – celestial and terrestrial. He lives in the *political community*, where he regards himself as a *communal being*, and in *civil society* where he acts simply as a *private individual*, treats other men as means, degrades himself to the role of a mere means, and becomes the plaything of alien powers. The political state, in relation to civil society, is just as spiritual as is heaven in relation to earth. It stands in the same opposition to civil society, and overcomes it in the same manner as religion overcomes the narrowness of the profane world; i.e. it has always to acknowledge it again, re-establish it, and allow itself to be dominated by it. Man, in his *most intimate* reality, in civil society, is a profane being. Here, where he appears both to himself and to others as a real individual he is an *illusory* phenomenon. In the state, on the contrary, where he is regarded as a species-being, man is the imaginary member of an imaginary sovereignty, divested of his real, individual life, and infused with an unreal universality.

'Bruno Bauer, "Die Judenfrage".' E.W., pp. 13–14

[Marx taught that the history of states (as of laws, codes, ideas and other elements of the superstructure) reflects the history of class struggles and of class domination. But he added that in some cases the state did not represent the rule of a single class. The earliest known state had purely administrative functions. Also, under the Asiatic mode of production the state is not an instrument of class rule. These two propositions appear contradictory. Possibly Marx meant that where class rule does exist, there the state will be at the service of the ruling class.

Nevertheless, two passages which appear on the same page of *The Eighteenth Brumaire of Louis Bonaparte* emphasise the apparent contradiction. Marx writes: 'Only under the second Bonaparte does the state seem to have made itself completely independent.' But later he adds: 'And yet the state power is not suspended in mid-air. Bonaparte represents a class . . . the small-holding peasants.']

This crystallisation of social activity, this consolidation of what we ourselves produce into an objective power above us, growing out of our control, thwarting our expectations, bringing to naught our calculations, is one of the chief factors in historical development up till now. And out of this very contradiction between the interest of the individual and that of the community the latter takes an independent form as the STATE, divorced from the real interests of individual and community, and at the same time as an illusory communal life, always based, however, on the real ties existing in every family and tribal conglomeration (such as flesh and blood, language, division of labour on a larger scale, and other interests) and especially, as we shall enlarge upon later, on the classes, already determined by the division of labour, which in every such mass of men separate out, and of which one dominates all the others. It follows from this that all struggles within the State, the struggle between democracy, aristocracy and monarchy, the struggle for the franchise, etc., etc., are merely the illusory forms in which the real struggles of the different classes are fought out among one another . . .

G.I., pp. 22–23

Since the State is the form in which the individuals of a ruling class assert their common interests, and in which the whole civil society of an epoch is epitomised, it follows that in the formation of all communal institutions the State acts as intermediary, that these institutions receive a political form. Hence the illusion that law is based on the will, and indeed on the will divorced from its real basis – on free will. Similarly, the theory of law is in its turn reduced to the actual laws.

G.I., p. 60

. . . The independence of the State is only found nowadays in those countries where the estates have not yet completely developed into classes, where the estates, done away with in more advanced countries, still have a part to play, and where there exists a mixture; countries, that is to say in which no one section of the population can achieve dominance over the others. This is the case particularly in Germany. The most perfect example of the modern State is North America. . . .

G.I., pp. 59–60

Truly, one must be destitute of all historical knowledge not to know that it is the sovereigns who in all ages have been subject to economic conditions, but they have never dictated laws to them. Legislation, whether political or civil, never does more than proclaim, express in words, the will of economic relations.

P.P., p. 83

[Marx demonstrated how to analyse contemporary events in the light of dialectical materialism in three brilliant essays, *The Class Struggles in France, 1848–50*, *The Eighteenth Brumaire of Louis Bonaparte* and *The Civil War in France*. Marx and Engels regarded France as the 'typical' nation as far as political history was concerned, and England as 'typical' in respect of economic development. (But since Marx emphasised the correlation of economic and political developments, this distinction is hard to assimilate.)

Marx portrays the July Monarchy as a class state in an unusual sense. Normally the ruling class does not in modern times attempt to make money out of the state machine itself, as occurred under Louis Philippe, but merely uses it to maintain the *status quo* and to suppress rebellion.]

The overthrow of the ministry of the coalition and the appearance of the ministry of the clerks had a second significance.* Its finance minister was *Fould*. Fould as finance minister signifies the official surrender of France's national wealth to the Bourse, the management of the state's property by the Bourse and in the

* Marx is here discussing the revolution of 1848 in France. Ed.

interests of the Bourse. With the nomination of Fould, the finance aristocracy announced its restoration in the *Moniteur*. This restoration necessarily supplemented the other restorations, which form just so many links in the chain of the constitutional republic.

Louis Philippe* had never dared to make a genuine *loup-cervier* (stock exchange shark) finance minister. Just as his monarchy was the ideal name for the rule of the big bourgeoisie, so in his ministries the privileged interests had to bear ideologically disinterested names. The bourgeois republic everywhere pushed into the forefront with the different monarchies, Legitimist as well as Orleanist, kept concealed in the background. It made earthly what they had made heavenly. In place of the names of the saints it put the bourgeois proper names of the dominant class interests.

Our whole exposition has shown how the republic, from the first day of its existence, did not overthrow but consolidated the finance aristocracy. But the concessions that were made to it were a fate to which submission was made without the desire to bring it about. With Fould, the initiative in the government returned to the finance aristocracy.

The question will be asked, how the coalesced bourgeoisie could bear and suffer the rule of finance, which under Louis Philippe depended on the exclusion or subordination of the remaining bourgeois factions.

The answer is simple.

First of all, the finance aristocracy itself forms a weighty, authoritative part of the royalist coalition, whose common governmental power is denominated republic Are not the spokesmen and leading lights among the Orleanists the old confederates and accomplices of the finance aristocracy? Is it not itself the golden phalanx of Orleanism? As far as the Legitimists are concerned, they had participated in practice already under Louis Philippe in all the orgies of the Bourse, mine and railway speculations. In general, the combination of large landed property with high finance is a *normal fact*. Proof: *England*: proof: even *Austria*

In a country like France, where the volume of national production stands at a disproportionately lower level than the

* King of the French, 1830–48. Ed

amount of the national debt, where government bonds form the most important subject of speculation and the Bourse the chief market for the investment of capital that wants to turn itself to account in an unproductive way – in such a country a countless number of people from all bourgeois or semi-bourgeois classes must have an interest in the state debt, in the Bourse gamblings, in finance. Do not all these interested subalterns find their natural mainstays and commanders in the faction which represents this interest in its vastest outlines, which represents it as a whole?

By what is the accrual of state property to high finance conditioned? By the constantly growing indebtedness of the state. And the indebtedness of the state? By the constant excess of its expenditure over its income, a disproportion which is simultaneously the cause and effect of the system of state loans.

In order to escape from his indebtedness, the state must either restrict its expenditure, that is, simplify and curtail the government organism, govern as little as possible, employ as small a personnel as possible, enter as little as possible into relations with bourgeois society. This path was impossible for the party of Order, whose means of repression, whose official interference in the name of the state and whose ubiquity through organs of state were bound to increase in the same measure as the number of quarters increased from which its rule and the conditions for the existence of its class were threatened. The *gendarmerie* cannot be reduced in the same measure as attacks on persons and property increase.

Or the state must seek to evade the debts and produce an immediate but transitory balance in its budget by putting *extraordinary taxes* on the shoulders of the wealthiest classes. But was the party of Order to sacrifice its own wealth on the altar of the fatherland in order to stop the national wealth from being exploited by the Bourse? *Pas si bête!*

Therefore, without a complete revolution in the French state, no revolution in the French state budget. Along with this state budget necessarily goes state indebtedness, and with state indebtedness necessarily goes the lordship of the trade in state debts, of the state creditors, the bankers, the money dealers and the wolves of the Bourse. Only one faction of the party of Order was directly concerned in the overthrow of the finance aristocracy – the *manufacturers*. We are not speaking of the middle, of the smaller people engaged in industry; we are speaking of the reigning princes of the manufacturing interests, who had formed the broad basis of the dynastic opposition under Louis Philippe. Their interest is indubitably reduction of the costs of production and hence reduction of the taxes, which enter into production, and hence reduction of the state debts, the interest on which enters into the taxes, hence the overthrow of the finance aristocracy.

In England – and the largest French manufacturers are petty bourgeois compared with their English rivals – we really find the manufacturers, a Cobden, a Bright, at the head of the crusade against the bank and the stock-exchange aristocracy. Why not in France? In England industry predominates; in France, agriculture. In England industry requires free trade; in France protective tariffs, national monopoly alongside of the other monopolies. French industry does not dominate French production; the French industrialists therefore, do not dominate the French bourgeoisie. In order to secure the advancement of their interests as against the remaining factions of the bourgeoisie, they cannot, like the English, take the lead of the movement and simultaneously push their class interests to the fore; they must follow in the train of the revolution, and serve interests which are opposed to the collective interests of their class. In February they had misunderstood their position; February sharpened their wits. And who is more directly threatened by the workers than the employer, the industrial capitalist? The manufacturer, therefore, of necessity became in France the most fanatical member of the party of Order. The reduction of his *profit* by finance, *what is that compared with the abolition of profit by the proletariat?*
The Class Struggles in France, 1848–50. S.W.I., pp. 208–11

. . . Under the Bourbons, *big landed property* had governed, with its priests and lackeys; under the Orleans, high finance, large-scale industry, large-scale trade, that is, *capital*, with its retinue of lawyers, professors and smooth-tongued orators. The Legitimate Monarchy was merely the political expression of the hereditary rule of the lords of the soil, as the July

Monarchy* was only the political expression of the usurped rule of the bourgeois *parvenus*. What kept the two factions apart, therefore, was not any so-called principles, it was their material conditions of existence, two different kinds of property, it was the old contrast between town and country, the rivalry between capital and landed property. That at the same time old memories, personal enmities, fears and hopes, prejudices and illusions, sympathies and antipathies, convictions, articles of faith and principles bound them to one or the other royal house, who is there that denies this? Upon the different forms of property, upon the social conditions of existence, rises an entire superstructure of distinct and peculiarly formed sentiments, illusions, modes of thought and views of life. The entire class creates and forms them out of its material foundations and out of the corresponding social relations. The single individual who derives them through tradition and upbringing, may imagine that they form the real motives and the starting-point of his activity. While Orleanists and Legitimists, while each faction sought to make itself and the other believe that it was loyalty to their two royal houses which separated them, facts later proved that it was rather their divided interests which forbade the uniting of the two royal houses. And as in private life one differentiates between what a man thinks and says of himself and what he really is and does, so in historical struggles one must distinguish still more the phrases and fancies of parties from their real organism and their real interests, their conception of themselves, from their reality. . . . Thus the Tories in England long imagined that they were enthusiastic about monarchy, the church and the beauties of the old English Constitution, until the day of danger wrung from them the confession that they are enthusiastic only about *ground rent*.

The 18th Brumaire of Louis Bonaparte. S.W.1., pp. 272-3

But let there be no misunderstanding. The Bonaparte dynasty represents not the revolutionary, but the conservative peasant; not the peasant that strikes out beyond the condition of his social existence, the small holding, but rather the peasant who wants to consolidate this holding, not the country folk who,

* Of 1830–1848. Ed.

linked up with the towns, want to overthrow the old order through their own energies, but on the contrary those who, in stupefied seclusion within this old order, want to see themselves and their small holdings saved and favoured by the ghost of the empire. It represents not the enlightenment, but the super-stition of the peasant; not his judgment, but his prejudice; not his future, but his past; not his modern Cevennes,* but his modern Vendée.†

The 18th Brumaire of Louis Bonaparte.   S.W.i., p. 335

The centralised State power, with its ubiquitous organs of standing army, police, bureaucracy, clergy, and judicature – organs wrought after the plan of a systematic and hierarchic division of labour – originates from the days of absolute monarchy, serving nascent middle-class society as a mighty weapon in its struggles against feudalism, Still, its development remained clogged by all manner of mediaeval rubbish, seignorial rights, local privileges, municipal and guild monopolies and provincial constitutions. The gigantic broom of the French Revolution of the eighteenth century swept away all these relics of bygone times, thus clearing simultaneously the social soil of its last hindrances to the superstructure of the modern State edifice raised under the First Empire, itself the offspring of the coalition wars of old semi-feudal Europe against modern France. During the subsequent *régimes* the Government, placed under parliamentary control – that is, under the direct control of the propertied classes – became not only a hotbed of huge national debts and crushing taxes; with its irresistible allurements of place, pelf, and patronage, it became not only the bone of contention between the rival factions and adventurers of the ruling classes; but its political character changed simultaneously with the economic changes of society. At the same pace at which the progress of modern industry developed, widened, intensified the class antagonism between capital and labour, the State power assumed more and more the character of the national

* The mountainous region of France where early in the 18th century there took place a large uprising of Protestant peasants demanding freedom of conscience and an end to arbitrary taxation.

† A region in the west of France which was a seat of Catholic and counter-revolutionary action during the French Revolution. Ed.

power of capital over labour, of a public force organised for social enslavement, of an engine of class despotism. After every revolution marking a progressive phase in the class struggle, the purely repressive character of the State power stands out in bolder and bolder relief. The Revolution of 1830, resulting in the transfer of Government from the landlords to the capitalists, transferred it from the more remote to the more direct antagonists of the working men. The bourgeois Republicans, who, in the name of the Revolution of February,* took the State power, used it for the June massacres,† in order to convince the working class that 'social' republic meant the Republic ensuring their social subjection, and in order to convince the royalist bulk of the bourgeois and landlord class that they might safely leave the cares and emoluments of Government to the bourgeois 'Republicans'. However, after their one heroic exploit of June, the bourgeois Republicans had, from the front, to fall back to the rear of the 'Party of Order' – a combination formed by all the rival fractions and factions of the appropriating class in their now openly declared antagonism to the producing classes. The proper form of their joint-stock Government was the *Parliamentary Republic*, with Louis Bonaparte for its President. Theirs was a *régime* of avowed class terrorism and deliberate insult towards the 'vile multitude'. If the Parliamentary Republic, as M. Thiers said, 'divided them (the different fractions of the ruling class) least,' it opened an abyss between that class and the whole body of society outside their spare ranks. The restraints by which their own divisions had under former *régimes* still checked the State power, were removed by their union; and in view of the threatening upheaval of the proletariat, they now used that State power mercilessly and ostentatiously as the national war-engine of capital against labour. In their uninterrupted crusade against the producing masses they were, however, bound not only to invest the executive with continually increased powers of repression, but at the same time to divest their own parliamentary stronghold – the National Assembly – one by one, of all its own means of defence against the Executive. The Executive, in the person of Louis Bonaparte, turned them

* Of 1848. Ed.

† Marx refers to the suppression of the working-class rising in Paris in June 1848. Ed.

out. The natural offspring of the 'Party-of-Order' Republic was the Second Empire.*

The empire, with the *coup d'état* for its certificate of birth, universal suffrage for its sanction, and the sword for its sceptre, professed to rest upon the peasantry, the large mass of producers not directly involved in the struggle of capital and labour. It professed to save the working class by breaking down Parliamentarism, and, with it, the undisguised subserviency of Government to the propertied classes. It professed to save the propertied classes by upholding their economic supremacy over the working class; and, finally, it professed to unite all classes by reviving for all the chimera of national glory. In reality, it was the only form of government possible at a time when the bourgeoisie had already lost, and the working class had not yet acquired, the faculty of ruling the nation. It was acclaimed throughout the world as the saviour of society. Under its sway, bourgeois society, freed from political cares, attained a development unexpected even by itself. Its industry and commerce expanded to colossal dimensions; financial swindling celebrated cosmopolitan orgies; the misery of the masses was set off by a shameless display of gorgeous, meretricious and debased luxury. The State power, apparently soaring high above society, was at the same time itself the greatest scandal of that society and the very hotbed of all its corruptions. Its own rottenness, and the rottenness of the society it had saved, were laid bare by the bayonet of Prussia, herself eagerly bent upon transferring the supreme seat of that *régime* from Paris to Berlin. Imperialism is, at the same time, the most prostitute and the ultimate form of the State power which nascent middle-class society had commenced to elaborate as a means of its own emancipation from feudalism, and which full-grown bourgeois society had finally transformed into a means for the enslavement of labour by capital.

The Civil War in France. S.W.I., pp. 516–18

With the beginning of March† the agitation for the election of the *Legislative National Assembly* had commenced. Two main

* Which replaced the Republic in 1852. Ed.

† Of 1849. Ed.

groups opposed each other, the *party of Order* and the *democratic-socialist*, or *Red, party*; between the two stood the *Friends of the Constitution*, under which name the tricolour republicans of the *National** sought to put forward a party. The *party of Order* was formed directly after the June days; only after December 10† had allowed it to cast off the coterie of the *National*, of the bourgeois republicans, was the secret of its existence, the *coalition* of *Orleanists* and *Legitimists* into *one party*, disclosed. The bourgeois class fell apart into two big factions, which, alternately, the *big landed proprietors* under the *restored monarchy* and the *finance aristocracy* and the *industrial bourgeoisie* under the *July monarchy*, had maintained a monopoly of power. *Bourbon* was the royal name for the predominant influence of the interests of the one faction, *Orleans* the royal name for the predominant influence of the interests of the other faction – the *nameless realm of the republic* was the only one in which both factions could maintain with equal power the common class interest without giving up their mutual rivalry. If the bourgeois republic could not be anything but the perfected and clearly expressed rule of the whole bourgeois class, could it be anything but the rule of the Orleanists supplemented by the Legitimists, and of the Legitimists supplemented by the Orleanists, the *synthesis of the restoration and the July monarchy*? The bourgeois republicans of the *National* did not represent any large faction of their class resting on economic foundations. They possessed only the importance and the historical claim of having asserted, under the monarchy, as against the two bourgeois factions that only understood their *particular régime*, the general régime of the bourgeois class, the *nameless realm of the republic*, which they idealised and embellished with antique arabesques, but in which, above all, they hailed the rule of their coterie. If the party of the *National* grew confused in its own mind when it described the royalists in coalition at the top of the republic founded by it, these royalists deceived themselves no less concerning the fact of their united rule. They did not comprehend that if each of their factions, regarded separately, by itself, was royalist, the product of their chemical combination

*A moderate Republican newspaper. Ed.

† Marx refers to 10 December 1848, the date of the election of Louis Bonaparte as President. Ed.

had necessarily to be *republican*, that the white and the blue monarchy had to neutralise each other in the tricolour republic. Forced, by antagonism to the revolutionary proletariat and the transition classes thronging more and more round it as their centre, to summon their united strength and to conserve the organisation of this united strength, each faction of the party of Order had to assert, as against the desire for restoration and the overweening presumption of the other, their joint rule, that is, the *republican form* of bourgeois rule. Thus we find these royalists in the beginning believing in an immediate restoration, later preserving the republican form with foaming rage and deadly invective against it on their lips, and finally confessing that they can endure each other only in the republic and postponing the restoration indefinitely. The enjoyment of the united rule itself strengthened each of the two factions, and made each of them still more unable and unwilling to subordinate itself to the other, that is, to restore the monarchy.

The *party of Order* directly proclaimed in its election programme the rule of the bourgeois class, that is, the preservation of the life conditions of its rule: *property, family, religion, order*! Naturally it represented its class rule and the conditions of *its* class rule as the rule of civilisation and as the necessary conditions of material production as well as of the relations of social intercourse arising from it. The party of Order had enormous money resources at its command; it organised its branches throughout France; it had all the ideologists of the old society in its pay; it had the influence of the existing governmental power at its disposal; it possessed an army of unpaid vassals in the whole mass of petty bourgeois and peasants, who, still removed from the revolutionary movement, found in the high dignitaries of property the natural representatives of their petty property and its petty prejudices. This party, represented throughout the country by countless petty kings, could punish the rejection of their candidates as insurrection, dismiss the rebellious workers, the recalcitrant farm-hands, domestic servants, railway officials, penmen, all the functionaries, civilly subordinate to it. Finally, here and there, it could maintain the delusion that the republican Constituent Assembly had prevented the Bonaparte of December 10 from manifesting his wonder-working powers. We have not mentioned the Bonapartists in connection with the party of

Order. They were not a serious faction of the bourgeois class, but a collection of old, superstitious invalids and of young, unbelieving soldiers of fortune. The party of Order was victorious in the elections; it sent a large majority into the Legislative Assembly.

As against the coalesced counter-revolutionary bourgeois class, the sections of the petty bourgeoisie and peasant class already revolutionised had naturally to ally themselves with the high dignitary of revolutionary interests, the revolutionary proletariat. We have seen how the democratic spokesmen of the petty bourgeoisie in parliament, that is, the *Montagne*, were driven by parliamentary defeats to the socialist spokesmen of the proletariat, and how the actual petty bourgeoisie, outside of parliament, was driven by the *concordats à l'amiable*, by the brutal enforcement of bourgeois interests and by bankruptcy, to the actual proletarians. On January 27, *Montagne* and Socialists had celebrated their reconciliation; at the great banquet of February 1849, they repeated their act of union. The social and democratic party, the party of the workers and that of the petty bourgeois, united to form the *social-democratic party*, that is, the *Red* party.

The Class Struggles in France, 1848–50.   S.W.1., pp. 189–91

The army itself was infected with the revolutionary fever. In voting for Bonaparte it had voted for victory, and he gave it defeat. In him it had voted for the Little Corporal, behind whom the great revolutionary general is concealed, and he once more gave it the great generals, behind whom the pipe-clay corporal shelters himself. There was no doubt that the Red party, that is, the coalesced democratic party, was bound to celebrate, if not victory, still, great triumphs; that Paris, the army and a great part of the provinces would vote for it. *Ledru-Rollin*, the leader of the *Montagne*, was elected by five Departments; no leader of the party of Order carried off such a victory, no candidate belonging to the proletarian party proper. This election reveals to us the secret of the democratic-socialist party. If, on the one hand, the *Montagne*, the parliamentary champion of the democratic petty bourgeoisie, was forced to unite with the socialist doctrinaires of the proletariat – the proletariat, forced by the terrible material defeat of June to raise itself up again through intellectual victories and not yet enabled through the development of the remaining classes to seize the revolutionary dictatorship, had to throw itself into the arms of the doctrinaires of its emancipation, the founders of socialist sects – the revolutionary peasants, the army and the provinces, on the other hand, ranged themselves behind the *Montagne*, which thus became the lord and master in the revolutionary army camp and through the understanding with the Socialists had eliminated every antagonism in the revolutionary party. In the latter half of the life of the Constituent Assembly it represented the republican fervour of the same and caused to be buried in oblivion its sins during the Provisional Government, during the Executive Commission, during the June days. In the same measure as the party of the *National*, in accordance with its half-and-half nature, had allowed itself to be put down by the royalist ministry, the party of the Mountain, which had been brushed aside during the omnipotence of the *National*, rose and asserted itself as the parliamentary representative of the revolution. In fact, the party of the *National* had nothing to oppose to the other, royalist factions but ambitious personalities and idealistic humbug. The party of the Mountain, on the contrary, represented a mass hovering between the bourgeoisie and the proletariat, a mass whose material interests demanded democratic institutions. In comparison with the Cavaignacs and the Marrasts, Ledru-Rollin and the *Montagne*, therefore, represented the true revolution, and from the consciousness of this important situation they drew the greater courage the more the expression of revolutionary energy limited itself to parliamentary attacks, bringing in bills of impeachment, threats, raised voices, thundering speeches, and extremes which were only pushed as far as phrases. The peasants were in about the same position as the petty bourgeoisie; they had more or less the same social demands to put forward. All the middle strata of society, so far as they were driven into the revolutionary movement, were therefore bound to find their hero in Ledru-Rollin. Ledru-Rollin was the personage of the democratic petty bourgeoisie. As against the party of Order, the half conservative, half revolutionary and wholly utopian reforms of this order had first to be pushed to the forefront.

On May 28,* the Legislative Assembly convened; on June 11, the collision of May 8 was renewed and, in the name of the *Montagne*, Ledru-Rollin brought in a bill of impeachment against the President and the ministry for violation of the constitution, for the bombardment of Rome. On June 12, the Legislative Assembly rejected the bill of impeachment, just as the Constituent Assembly had rejected it on May 11, but the proletariat this time drove the *Montagne* on to the streets, not to a street battle, however, but only to a street procession. It is enough to say that the *Montagne* was at the head of this movement to know that the movement was defeated, and that June 1849 was a caricature, as ridiculous as it was vile, of June 1848. The great retreat of June 13* was only eclipsed by the still greater battle report of Changarnier, the great man that the party of Order improvised. Every social epoch needs its great men, and when it does not find them, it invents them, as Helvétius says.

On December 20† only one half of the constituted bourgeois republic was in existence, the *President*; on May 28‡ it was completed by the other half, the *Legislative Assembly*. In June 1848, the constituent bourgeois republic, by an unspeakable battle against the proletariat, and in June 1849, the constituted bourgeois republic, by an unutterable comedy with the petty bourgeoisie, had engraved their names in the birth register of history. June 1849 was the Nemesis of June 1848. In June 1849, it was not the workers that were vanquished; it was the petty bourgeois, who stood between them and the revolution, that were felled. June 1849 was not a bloody tragedy between wage labour and capital, but a prison-filling and lamentable play of debtors and creditors. The party of Order had won, it was all-powerful; it had now to show what it was.

> The Class Struggles in France, 1848–50.
> S.W.I., pp. 192–5

* 1849. Ed.
† 1848. Ed.
‡ 1849. Ed.

B. The Workers' Movement

MANIFESTO OF THE COMMUNIST PARTY

A spectre is haunting Europe – the spectre of Communism. All the Powers of old Europe have entered into a holy alliance to exorcise this spectre: Pope and Czar, Metternich and Guizot, French Radicals and German police-spies.

Where is the party in opposition that has not been decried as Communistic by its opponents in power? Where the Opposition that has not hurled back the branding reproach of Communism, against the more advanced opposition parties, as well as against its reactionary adversaries?

Two things result from this fact.

I. Communism is already acknowledged by all European Powers to be itself a Power.

II. It is high time that Communists should openly, in the face of the whole world, publish their views, their aims, their tendencies, and meet this nursery tale of the Spectre of Communism with a Manifesto of the party itself.

To this end, Communists of various nationalities have assembled in London, and sketched the following Manifesto, to be published in the English, French, German, Italian, Flemish and Danish languages.

C.M., p. 44

The Communists, therefore, are on the one hand, practically, the most advanced and resolute section of the working-class parties of every country, that section which pushes forward all others; on the other hand, theoretically, they have over the great mass of the proletariat the advantage of clearly understanding the line of march, the conditions, and the ultimate general results of the proletarian movement.

The immediate aim of the Communists is the same as that of all the other proletarian parties: formation of the proletariat into a class, overthrow of the bourgeois supremacy, conquest of political power by the proletariat.

The theoretical conclusions of the Communists are in no way based on ideas or principles that have been invented, or discovered, by this or that would-be universal reformer.

They merely express, in general terms, actual relations springing from an existing class struggle, from a historical movement going on under our very eyes. The abolition of existing property relations is not at all a distinctive feature of Communism.

C.M., p. 70

[As active revolutionaries, Marx and Engels became members of the League of Communists and the Universal Society of Revolutionary Communists, where they collaborated with the French followers of Auguste Blanqui and with revolutionary English Chartists like Harney. These small groups of predominantly exiled intellectuals lacked genuine roots in the working-class movement. Consequently they tended to think in terms of conspiratorial *coups*. Engels later described 1848 as a 'time of surprise attacks, of revolutions carried through by small conscious minorities at the head of unconscious masses . . .'

After 1850 Marx broke entirely with these groups. He now saw the need for a broad-based, long-term workers' movement, independent of all bourgeois influence. Exiled in London, he turned hopefully towards the English trade unions.]

In England they have not stopped at partial combinations which have no other objective than a passing strike, and which disappear with it. Permanent combinations have been formed, *trades unions*, which serve as ramparts for the workers in their struggles with the employers. And at the present time all these local *trades unions* find a rallying point in the *National Association of United Trades*, the central committee of which is in London, and which already numbers 80,000 members. The organisation of these strikes, combinations, and *trades unions* went on simultaneously with the political struggles of the workers, who now constitute a large political party, under the name of Chartists.

The first attempts of workers to *associate* among themselves always takes place in the form of combinations.

Large-scale industry concentrates in one place a crowd of people unknown to one another. Competition divides their interests. But the maintenance of wages, this common interest which they have against their boss, unites them in a common thought of resistance – *combination*. Thus combination always has a double aim, that of stopping competition among the workers, so that they can carry on general competition with the capitalist. If the first aim of resistance was merely the maintenance of wages, combinations, at first isolated, constitute themselves into groups as the capitalists in their turn unite for the purpose of repression, and in face of always united capital, the maintenance of the association becomes more necessary to them than that of wages. This is so true that English economists are amazed to see the workers sacrifice a good part of their wages in favour of associations, which, in the eyes of these economists, are established solely in favour of wages. In this struggle – a veritable civil war – all the elements necessary for a coming battle unite and develop. Once it has reached this point, association takes on a political character.

P.P. pp. 172–3

The proletariat goes through various stages of development. With its birth begins its struggle with the bourgeoisie. At first the contest is carried on by individual labourers, then by the workpeople of a factory, then by the operatives of one trade, in one locality, against the individual bourgeois who directly exploits them. They direct their attacks not against the bourgeois conditions of production, but against the instruments of production themselves; they destroy imported wares that compete with their labour, they smash to pieces machinery, they set factories ablaze, they seek to restore by force the vanished status of the workman of the Middle Ages.

At this stage the labourers still form an incoherent mass scattered over the whole country, and broken up by their mutual competition. If anywhere they unite to form more compact bodies, this is not yet the consequence of their own active union, but of the union of the bourgeoisie, which class, in order to attain its own political ends, is compelled to set the whole proletariat in motion, and is moreover yet, for a time, able to do so. At this stage, therefore, the proletarians do not fight their enemies, but the enemies of their enemies, the remnants of absolute monarchy, the landowners, the non-industrial bourgeois, the petty bourgeoisie. Thus the whole historical movement is concentrated in the hands of the bourgeoisie; every victory so obtained is a victory for the bourgeoisie.

But with the development of industry the proletariat not only increases in number; it becomes concentrated in greater masses, its strength grows, and it feels that strength more. The various interests and conditions of life within the ranks of the proletariat are more and more equalised, in proportion as machinery obliterates all distinctions of labour, and nearly everywhere reduces wages to the same low level. The growing competition among the bourgeois, and the resulting commercial crises, make the wages of the workers ever more fluctuating. The unceasing improvement of machinery, ever more rapidly developing, makes their livelihood more and more precarious; the collisions between individual workmen and individual bourgeois take more and more the character of collisions between two classes. Thereupon the workers begin to form combinations (Trades' Unions) against the bourgeois; they club together in order to keep up the rate of wages; they found permanent associations in order to make provision beforehand for these occasional revolts. Here and there the contest breaks out into riots.

Now and then the workers are victorious, but only for a time. The real fruit of their battles lies, not in the immediate result, but in the ever-expanding union of the workers. . . .

This organisation of the proletarians into a class, and consequently into a political party, is continually being upset again by the competition between the workers themselves. But it ever rises up again, stronger, firmer, mightier. It compels legislative recognition of particular interests of the workers, by taking advantage of the divisions among the bourgeoisie itself. Thus the ten-hours' bill in England was carried.

C.M., pp. 60–62

These few hints will suffice to show that the very development of modern industry must progressively turn the scale in favour of the capitalist against the working man, and that consequently the general tendency of capitalistic production is not to raise, but to sink the average standard of wages, or to push the *value of labour* more or less to its *minimum limit*. Such being the tendency of *things* in this system, is this saying that the working class ought to renounce their resistance against the encroachments of capital, and abandon their attempts at making the best of the occasional chances for their temporary improvement? If they did, they would be degraded to one level mass of broken wretches past salvation. I think I have shown that their struggles for the standard of wages are incidents inseparable from the whole wages system, that in 99 cases out of 100 their efforts at raising wages are only efforts at maintaining the given value of labour, and that the necessity of debating their price with the capitalist is inherent in their condition of having to sell themselves as commodities. By cowardly giving way in their everyday conflict with capital, they would certainly disqualify themselves for the initiating of any larger movement.

Wages, Price and Profit. S.W.I., p. 446

[Unceasingly as Marx urged the workers and their unions to fight for higher wages and a shorter working day, he equally warned them not to fall into a reformist frame of mind. The evils of capitalism could be dispelled only by a revolutionary overthrow of the entire system. There is no logical inconsistency in this double tactic, but it was destined to throw an immense psychological strain on the Marxist parties of the Second International in the thirty years preceding the First World War.]

At the same time, and quite apart from the general servitude involved in the wages system, the working class ought not to exaggerate to themselves the ultimate working of these everyday struggles. They ought not to forget that they are fighting with effects, but not with the causes of those effects; that they are retarding the downward movement, but not changing its direction; that they are applying palliatives, not curing the malady. They ought, therefore, not to be exclusively absorbed in these unavoidable guerilla fights incessantly springing up from the never-ceasing encroachments of capital or changes of the market. They ought to understand that, with all the miseries it imposes upon them, the present system simultaneously engenders the *material conditions* and the *social forms* necessary for an economical reconstruction of society. Instead of the *conservative* motto, '*A fair day's wage for a fair day's work!*' they ought to inscribe on their banner the *revolutionary* watchword, '*Abolition of the wages system!*'

Wages, Price and Profit. S.W.I., p. 446

On the other hand, however, every movement in which the working class comes out as a *class* against the ruling classes and tries to coerce them by pressure from without is a political movement. For instance, the attempt in a particular factory or even in a particular trade to force a shorter working day out of individual capitalists by strikes, etc., is a purely economic movement. On the other hand the movement to force through an eight-hour, etc., *law*, is a *political* movement. And in this way, out of the separate economic movements of the workers there grows up everywhere a *political* movement, that is to say, a movement of the *class*, with the object of enforcing its interests in a general form, in a form possessing general, socially coercive force. While these movements presuppose a certain degree of previous organisation, they are in turn equally a means of developing this organisation.

Where the working class is not yet far enough advanced in its organisation to undertake a decisive campaign against the collective power, i.e., the political power of the ruling classes, it must at any rate be trained for this by continual agitation against this power and by a hostile attitude towards the policies of the ruling classes. Otherwise it remains a plaything in their hands, as the September revolution in France showed, and as is also proved to a certain extent by the game that Messrs. Gladstone & Co. have been successfully engaged in in England up to the present time.

Marx to F. Bolte, Nov. 23, 1871. S.C., pp. 328–9

[Marx was troubled by the fact that the most economically advanced and best organised working class – the English – was also among the most reformist. In stressing the importance of the Irish question in bringing this about, Marx was perhaps resisting the conclusion that rising wages and the quasi-democratic state had permanently destroyed the possibilities of revolution in England. In 1863 he wrote: 'How soon the English workers will free themselves from their apparent bourgeois infection one must wait and see.' By 1872 he had come to the conclusion that in England, the United States and perhaps Holland, the workers might attain power without a revolution, because of the democratic nature of these states. (Yet Marx had elsewhere described the democratic state as the purest form of class-dominated state.) Later he told H. M. Hyndman that a revolution in England was possible but not inevitable.]

I have become more and more convinced – and the only question is to drive this conviction home to the English working class – that it can never do anything decisive here in England until it separates its policy with regard to Ireland most definitely from the policy of the ruling classes, until it not only makes common cause with the Irish but actually takes the initiative in dissolving the Union established in 1801 and replacing it by a free federal relationship. And this must be done, not as a matter of sympathy with Ireland but as a demand made in the interests of the English proletariat. If not, the English people will remain tied to the leading-strings of the ruling classes, because it will have to join with them in a common front against Ireland. Every one of its movements in England itself is crippled by the strife with the Irish, who form a very important section of the working class in England. *The prime condition* of emancipation here – the overthrow of the English landed oligarchy – remains impossible because its position here cannot be stormed so long as it maintains its strongly entrenched outposts in Ireland. But there, once affairs are in the hands of the Irish people itself, once it is made its own legislator and ruler, once it becomes autonomous, the abolition of the landed aristocracy (to a large extent the *same persons* as the English landlords) will be infinitely easier than here, because in Ireland it is not merely a simple economic question but at the same time a *national* question, since the landlords there are not, like those in England, the traditional dignitaries and representatives of the nation, but its mortally hated oppressors. And not only does England's internal social development remain crippled by her present relations with Ireland; her foreign policy, and particularly her policy with regard to Russia and the United States of America, suffers the same fate.

But since the English working class undoubtedly throw the decisive weight into the scale of social emancipation generally, the lever has to be applied here. . . .

Marx to L. Kugelmann, Nov. 29, 1869.   S.C., p. 277

And most important of all! Every industrial and commercial centre in England now possesses a working class *divided* into two *hostile* camps, English proletarians and Irish proletarians. The ordinary English worker hates the Irish worker as a competitor who lowers his standard of life. In relation to the Irish worker he feels himself a member of the *ruling* nation and so turns himself into a tool of the aristocrats and capitalists of his country *against Ireland*, thus strengthening their domination *over himself.* He cherishes religious, social, and national prejudices against the Irish worker. His attitude towards him is much the same as that of the 'poor whites' to the 'niggers' in the former slave states of the U.S.A. The Irishman pays him back with interest in his own money. He sees in the English worker at once the accomplice and the stupid tool of the *English rule in Ireland.*

This antagonism is artificially kept alive and intensified by the press, the pulpit, the comic papers, in short, by all the means at the disposal of the ruling classes. This *antagonism* is the *secret of the impotence of the English working class,* despite its organisation. It is the secret by which the capitalist class maintains its power. And that class is fully aware of it.

But the evil does not stop here. It continues across the ocean. The antagonism between English and Irish is the hidden basis of the conflict between the United States and England. It makes any honest and serious co-operation between the working classes of the two countries impossible. It enables the governments of both countries, whenever they think fit, to break the edge off the social conflict by their mutual bullying, and, in case of need, by war with one another.

England, being the metropolis of capital, the power which has hitherto ruled the world market, is for the present the most important country for the workers' revolution, and moreover the *only* country in which the material conditions for this revolution have developed up to a certain degree of maturity. Therefore to hasten the social revolution in England is the most important object of the International Workingmen's Association. The sole means of hastening it is to make Ireland independent.

Hence it is the task of the International everywhere to put the conflict between England and Ireland in the foreground, and everywhere to side openly with Ireland. And it is the special task of the Central Council in London to awaken a consciousness in the English workers that *for them* the *national emancipation of Ireland* is no question of abstract justice or humanitarian sentiment but *the first condition of their own social emancipation.* Marx to S. Meyer and A. Vogt, April 9, 1870.   S.C.,

pp. 286–7

[Like Lenin after them, Marx and Engels rejected the idea of a broad-based workers' party embracing widely divergent ideological trends. This raises once again the paradox of working-class consciousness. On the one hand Marx argued that the predicament of the proletariat would naturally generate class-consciousness; on the other he saw that it was only by a great effort of energy and organisation that the workers could be saved from reformist or anarchist heresies. Marx reacted fiercely to all rivals, real or imaginary; his denunciations of Proudhon and Ferdinand Lassalle, who organised the first German workers' party in 1863, were unceasing. Marx yearned to reach the workers (although his writings make few concessions to less educated minds). In 1873 he wrote: 'The appreciation which *Das Kapital* rapidly gained in wide circles of the German working class is the best reward of my labours.']

Secondly. If people of this kind from other classes join the proletarian movement, the first condition must be that they should not bring any remnants of bourgeois, petty-bourgeois, etc., prejudices with them but should wholeheartedly adopt the proletarian outlook. But these gentlemen, as has been proved, are chock-full of bourgeois and petty bourgeois ideas. In such a petty-bourgeois country as Germany these ideas certainly have their justification. But only *outside* the Social-Democratic Workers' Party. If these gentlemen constitute themselves into a Social-Democratic petty-bourgeois party they have a perfect right to do so; one could then negotiate with them, form a *bloc* according to circumstances, etc. But in a workers' party they are an adulterating element. If reasons exist for tolerating them there for the moment it is our duty *only* to tolerate them, to allow them no influence in the Party leadership and to remain aware that a break with them is only a matter of time. That time, moreover, seems to have come. How the Party can tolerate the authors of this article in its midst any longer is incomprehensible to us. But if even the leadership of the Party should fall more or less into the hands of such people, the Party would simply be castrated and there would be an end of proletarian snap.

As for ourselves, in view of our whole past there is only one road open to us. For almost forty years we have stressed the class struggle as the immediate driving power of history, and in particular the class struggle between bourgeoisie and proletariat as the great lever of the modern social revolution; it is, therefore, impossible for us to co-operate with people who wish to expunge this class struggle from the movement. When the International was formed we expressly formulated the battle-cry: The emancipation of the working classes must be conquered by the working classes themselves. We cannot therefore co-operate with people who openly state that the workers are too un-educated to emancipate themselves and must be freed from above by philanthropic big bourgeois and petty bourgeois. If the new Party organ adopts a line that corresponds to the views of these gentlemen, that is bourgeois and not proletarian, then nothing remains for us, much though we should regret it, but publicly to declare our opposition to it, and to dissolve the bonds of the solidarity with which we have hitherto represented the German Party abroad. But it is to be hoped that things will not come to *such* a pass . . .

Marx and Engels, 'Circular Letter'
Sept. 17–18, 1879. S.C., pp. 394–5

'Yet once again,' in No. 16 of the *Social-Demokrat** where, bristling with misprints, my letter on Proudhon appears, Moses Hess,† for the second time 'all ready', *denounces* the 'International Association'. I wrote a furious letter about this to Liebknecht yesterday and told him that he had now had the *very last* warning; that I did not give a farthing for 'good intentions' which did the work of bad intentions; that I cannot get the members of the 'International Committee' here to understand that things of this kind are done in good faith out of sheer stupidity; that their filthy rag, while it continues to glorify Lassalle, although they know now what treachery he was secretly harbouring, and while it cravenly flirts with Bismarck, has the shamelessness to accuse us here, through the Plonplonist‡ Hess, of Plonplonism, etc.

Now, my opinion is as follows: We start from Moses' denunciation or insinuation in order first to get out in a few words a declaration of war against Bonaparte Plon-Plon, taking the opportunity to give honourable mention also to Moses' friend, the Rabbi Ein-Horn. We then use this to declare ditto against Bismarck and against the knaves or fools who dream or drivel about an alliance with him for the working class. . . .

Marx to Engels, Feb. 3, 1865. S.C., pp. 194–5

[In 1863–4 Marx emerged from a long period of withdrawal and theoretical work to become the guiding ideological spirit of the new International Working Men's Association – the

* Organ of the General Association of German Workers, founded by Marx's rival Lassalle. Ed.

† A 'True Socialist' who had influenced Marx and Engels in the early 1840's. Ed.

‡ 'Plon-Plon' – a cousin of Napoleon III. Ed.

First International. The IWMA established branches and attracted followers in France, England, Belgium and Switzerland, as well as a few converts in Germany, Italy and Spain. But Marx found it heavy going. Neither the English nor the French trade unionists who formed the backbone of the International were Marxists. In Marx's native Germany, Lassalle's ideas were dominant. After 1868, when Marx was forcing his ideas through at Congresses, Bakunin's revolutionary anarchism rapidly gained influence. The defeat of the Paris Commune in 1871 was virtually the deathblow to the International. But Marx rose] with this defiant challenge.

After Whit-Sunday, 1871, there can be neither peace nor truce possible between the working men of France and the appropriators of their produce. The iron hand of a mercenary soldiery may keep for a time both classes tied down in common oppression. But the battle must break out again and again in ever-growing dimensions, and there can be no doubt as to who will be the victor in the end – the appropriating few, or the immense working majority. And the French working class is only the advanced guard of the modern proletariat.

While the European governments thus testify, before Paris, to the international character of class-rule, they cry down the International Working Men's Association – the international counter-organisation of labour against the cosmopolitan conspiracy of capital – as the head fountain of all these disasters. Thiers denounced it as the despot of labour, pretending to be its liberator. Picard ordered that all communications between the French Internationals and those abroad should be cut off; Count Jaubert, Thiers' mummified accomplice of 1835, declares it the great problem of all civilised governments to weed it out. The Rurals roar against it, and the whole European press joins the chorus. An honourable French writer, completely foreign to our Association, speaks as follows: 'The members of the Central Committee of the National Guard, as well as the greater part of the members of the Commune, are the most active, intelligent, and energetic minds of the International Working Men's Association; . . . men who are thoroughly honest, sincere, intelligent, devoted, pure, and fanatical in the *good* sense of the word.' The police-tinged bourgeois mind naturally figures to itself the International Working Men's Association as acting in the manner of a secret conspiracy, its central body ordering, from time to time, explosions in different countries. Our Association is, in fact, nothing but the international bond between the most advanced working men in the various countries of the civilised world. Wherever, in whatever shape, and under whatever conditions the class struggle obtains any consistency, it is but natural that members of our Association should stand in the foreground. The soil out of which it grows is modern society itself. It cannot be stamped out by any amount of carnage. To stamp it out, the Governments would have to stamp out the despotism of capital over labour – the condition of their own parasitical existence.

Working men's Paris, with its Commune, will be for ever celebrated as the glorious harbinger of a new society. Its martyrs are enshrined in the great heart of the working class. Its exterminators, history has already nailed to that external pillory from which all the prayers of their priests will not avail to redeem them.

The Civil War in France. S.W.I, pp. 541–2

[Marx believed that the defeat of France by Prussia in 1870 would result in a shift of the centre of gravity of the working-class movement from France to Germany. It was in Germany that his own ideas were most likely to make progress.]

. . . If the German working class does not then play the historical role it is entitled to it will be its own fault. *This war has shifted the centre of gravity of the working-class movement on the Continent from France to Germany.* This places greater responsibility upon the German working class.

Marx to the Committee of the Social-
Democratic Workers' Party of Germany,
Brunswick, approx. Sept. 1, 1870. S.C., p. 301

C. Revolution

[The bourgeois revolution succeeds with the support of the masses. The masses subsequently become disillusioned and embittered on discovering that the generalised ideals proclaimed by the revolution were merely a mask for particular, bourgeois interests. The proletariat proceeds towards its own revolution.

Marx believed that violence had an immanent historical function. In *Capital* he wrote: 'Force is the midwife of every old society pregnant with a new one.']

. . The Revolution was a 'failure' only for the mass which did not find in the *political* 'idea' the idea of its real *'interest'*, whose real life-principle did not therefore coincide with the life-principle of the Revolution; the mass whose real conditions for emancipation were substantially different from the conditions within which the bourgeoisie could emancipate itself and society. If the revolution, which can exemplify all great historical 'actions' was a failure, it was so because the mass whose living conditions it did not substantially go beyond was an *exclusive*, *limited* mass, not an all-embracing one. If it was a failure it was not because it aroused the *'enthusiasm'* and *'interest'* of the mass, but because the most numerous part of the mass, the part most greatly differing from the bourgeoisie, did not find its *real* interest in the principle of the revolution, had no revolutionary principle of *its own*, but *only* an *'idea'*, and hence only an object of momentary *enthusiasm* and only apparent *exaltation*.

H.F., p. 110

This appropriation* is further determined by the manner in which it must be effected. It can only be effected through a union, which by the character of the proletariat itself can again only be a universal one, and through a revolution, in which on the one hand the power of the earlier mode of production and intercourse and social organisation is overthrown, and on the other hand there develops the universal character and the energy of the proletariat, without which the revolution cannot be accomplished; and in which, further, the proletariat rids itself of everything that still clings to it from its previous position in society.

G.I, p. 67

... In the development of productive forces there comes a stage at which productive forces and means of intercourse are called into existence, which, under the existing relationships, only cause mischief, and which are no longer productive but destructive forces (machinery and money); and connected with this a class is called forth, which has to bear all the burdens of society without enjoying its advantages, which, ousted from society, is forced into the most decided antagonism to all other classes; a class which forms the majority of all members of society, and from which emanates the consciousness of the necessity of a fundamental revolution, the communist consciousness, which may, of course, arise among the other classes too through the contemplation of the situation of this class. ...

G.I, pp. 68–69

... In all revolutions up till now the mode of activity always remained unscathed and it was only a question of a different distribution of this activity, a new distribution of labour to other persons, whilst the communistic revolution is directed against the preceding *mode* of activity, does away with *labour*, and abolishes the rule of all classes with the classes themselves, because it is carried through by the class which no longer counts

* Of the instruments of production by the workers. Ed.

as a class in society, is not recognised as a class, and is in itself the expression of the dissolution of all classes, nationalities, etc., within present society; and both for the production on a mass scale of this communist consciousness, and for the success of the cause itself, the alteration of men on a mass scale is necessary, an alteration which can only take place in a practical movement, a *revolution*; this revolution is necessary, therefore, not only because the ruling class cannot be overthrown in any other way, but also because the class *overthrowing* it can only in a revolution succeed in ridding itself of all the muck of ages and become fitted to found society anew.

G.I, p. 69

[Like other German communists in the 1840's, Marx believed that a bourgeois revolution in Germany might rapidly be followed by a proletarian one. The revolution would be 'permanent'. This prediction was upheld despite the backwardness of German industry and the relative weakness of the German proletariat.

Marx was undoubtedly mistaking the wish for the reality. However, his error apparently stemmed from an interesting conception of the role of political consciousness. Socialist ideas were now maturing – the product of French political development and of the English industrial revolution. This, Marx reasoned, endowed the German proletariat with a borrowed ideological maturity, a factor which might compensate for its physical disadvantages and enable it to accelerate the historical process.

But such a prediction ran counter to Marx's emphasis on the *long-term* development of capitalism as the necessary prelude to revolution.

In the event the factor of historical consciousness did intervene in 1848 – but in the reverse direction. Terrified of communism and remembering the events of 1789–94 in France, the German bourgeoisie refused to collaborate with the workers, as Marx had hoped they would. The bourgeoisie embraced the counter-revolution at the first sign of a popular rising.]

The Communists turn their attention chiefly to Germany, because that country is on the eve of a bourgeois revolution that is bound to be carried out under more advanced conditions of European civilisation, and with a much more developed proletariat, than that of England was in the seventeenth, and of France in the eighteenth century, and because the bourgeois revolution in Germany will be but the prelude to an immediately following proletarian revolution.   C.M., p. 107

The *Prussian March Revolution** must not be confused with the *English* Revolution of 1648 or the French of 1789.

In 1648† the bourgeoisie was allied with the modern nobility against the monarchy, against the feudal nobility and against the established church.

In 1789‡ the bourgeoisie was allied with the people against the monarchy, the nobility and the established church.

The Revolution of 1789 had as its prototype (at least in Europe) only the Revolution of 1648, and the Revolution of 1648 only the insurrection of the Netherlanders against Spain. Not only in time but also in content both revolutions were a century beyond their prototypes.

In both revolutions the bourgeoisie was the class that *really* formed the van of the movement. The *proletariat* and *the strata of the burghers which did not belong to the bourgeoisie* either had as yet no interests separate from those of the bourgeoisie or they did not yet constitute independently developed classes or subdivisions of classes. Hence where they came out in opposition to the bourgeoisie, as for instance in France in 1793 till 1794, they fought only for the realisation of the interests of the bourgeoisie, even if not *in the fashion* of the bourgeoisie. The *whole French terrorism* was nothing but a *plebeian manner* of settling accounts with the *enemies of the bourgeoisie*, with absolutism, feudalism and philistinism.

The Revolutions of 1648 and 1789 were not *English* and *French* revolutions; they were revolutions of a *European* pattern.

* Of 1848. Ed.
† In England. Ed.
‡ In France. Ed.

They were not the victory of a *definite* class of society over the *old political order*; they were the *proclamation of political order for the new European society.* The bourgeoisie was victorious in these revolutions; but the *victory of the bourgeoisie* was at that time the *victory of a new order of society*, the victory of bourgeois property over feudal property, of nationality over provincialism, of competition over the guild, or partition over primogeniture, of the owner of the land over the domination of the owner by the land, of enlightenment over superstition, of the family over the family name, of industry over heroic laziness, of civil law over medieval privilege. The Revolution of 1648 was the victory of the seventeenth century over the sixteenth century, the Revolution of 1789 the victory of the eighteenth century over the seventeenth century. These revolutions expressed still more the needs of the world of that day than of the sectors of the world in which they occurred, of England and France.

In the *March Revolution in Prussia* there was nothing of the kind.

The February Revolution* had *abolished* the constitutional monarchy in reality and the rule of the bourgeoisie in the mind. The March Revolution in Prussia was to *establish* the constitutional monarchy in the mind and the rule of the bourgeoisie in reality. Far from being a *European revolution* it was but the stunted after-effect of a European revolution in a backward country. Instead of being ahead of its age it trailed more than half a century behind it. It was *secondary* from the outset, but it is a known fact that secondary diseases are more difficult to cure and at the same time waste the body more than original diseases. It was not a question of the establishment of a new society but of the rebirth in Berlin of the society that had passed away in Paris. The March Revolution in Prussia was not even *national, German*; it was *provincial-Prussian* from its inception. The Vienna, Cassel, Munich and every other sort of provincial uprising swept on alongside of it and contested its lead.

While 1648 and 1789 had taken infinite pride in being the acme of creation it was the ambition of the Berlin of 1848 to form an anachronism. Their light was like the light of the stars which reaches us who dwell on earth only after the bodies which radiated it have been extinct for a hundred-thousand years. The

* In Paris. Ed.

March Revolution in Prussia was, in miniature – as it was every-thing in miniature – just such a star for Europe. Its light was the light of the corpse of a society that had long ago become putrified.

The German bourgeoisie had developed so slothfully, cravenly and slowly that at the moment when it menacingly faced feudalism and absolutism it saw itself menacingly faced by the proletariat and all factions of the burghers whose interests and ideas were akin to those of the proletariat. And it saw inimically arrayed not only a class *behind* it but all of Europe *before* it. The Prussian bourgeoisie was not, as the French of 1789 had been, the class which represented the *whole* of modern society *vis-à-vis* the representatives of the old society, the monarchy and the nobility. It had sunk to the level of a sort of *social estate*, as distinctly opposed to the crown as to the people, eager to be in the opposition to both, irresolute against each of its opponents, taken severally, because it always saw both of them before or behind it; inclined from the very beginning to betray the people and compromise with the crowned repre-sentative of the old society because it itself already belonged to the old society; . . .

The Bourgeoisie and the
Counter-Revolution.   S.W.I, pp. 67–69

In the first French Revolution the rule of the *Constitutionalists* is followed by the rule of the *Girondins* and the rule of the *Girondins* by the rule of the *Jacobins*. Each of these parties relies on the more progressive party for support. As soon as it has brought the revolution far enough to be unable to follow it further, still less to go ahead of it, it is thrust aside by the bolder ally that stands behind it and sent to the guillotine. The revolu-tion thus moves along an ascending line.

It is the reverse with the Revolution of 1848. The proletarian party appears as an appendage of the petty-bourgeois-democratic party. It is betrayed and dropped by the latter on April 16, May 15, and in the June days. The democratic party, in its turn, leans on the shoulders of the bourgeois-republican party. The bourgeois-republicans no sooner believe themselves well established than they shake off the troublesome comrade and support themselves on the shoulders of the party of Order. The party of Order hunches its shoulders, lets the bourgeois-republicans tumble and throws itself on the shoulders of armed force. It fancies it is still sitting on its shoulders when, one fine morning, it perceives that the shoulders have transformed themselves into bayonets. Each party kicks back at the one behind, which presses upon it, and leans against the one in front, which pushes backwards. No wonder that in this ridiculous posture it loses its balance and, having made the inevitable grimaces, collapses with curious capers. The revolution thus moves in a descending line. It finds itself in this state of retrogressive motion before the last February barricade has been cleared away and the first revolutionary authority constituted.

The 18th Brumaire of Louis Bonaparte. S.W.1., pp. 268–9

The development of the industrial proletariat is, in general, conditioned by the development of the industrial bourgeoisie. Only under its rule does the proletariat gain that extensive national existence which can raise its revolution to a national one, and does it itself create the modern means of production, which become just so many means of its revolutionary emancipation. Only its rule tears up the material roots of feudal society and levels the ground on which alone a proletarian revolution is possible. French industry is more developed and the French bourgeoisie more revolutionary than that of the rest of the Continent. But was not the February Revolution* levelled directly against the finance aristocracy? This fact proved that the industrial bourgeoisie did not rule France. The industrial bourgeoisie can rule only where modern industry shapes all property relations to suit itself, and industry can win this power only where it has conquered the world market, for national bounds are inadequate for its development. But French industry, to a great extent, maintains its command even of the national market only through a more or less modified system of prohibitive duties. While, therefore, the French proletariat, at the moment of a revolution, possesses in Paris actual power and influence which spur it on to a drive beyond its means, in the

* Of 1848, in Paris. Ed.

rest of France it is crowded into separate, scattered industrial centres, being almost lost in the superior numbers of peasants and petty bourgeois. The struggle against capital in its developed, modern form, in its decisive aspect, the struggle of the industrial wage-worker against the industrial bourgeois, is in France a partial phenomenon, which after the February days could so much the less supply the national content of the revolution, since the struggle against capital's secondary modes of exploitation, that of the peasant against usury and mortgages or of the petty bourgeois against the wholesale dealer, banker and manufacturer, in a word, against bankruptcy, was still hidden in the general uprising against the finance aristocracy. Nothing is more understandable, then, than that the Paris proletariat sought to secure the advancement of its own interests *side by side* with those of the bourgeoisie, instead of enforcing them as the revolutionary interests of society itself, that it let the *red* flag be lowered to the *tricolour*. The French workers could not take a step forward, could not touch a hair of the bourgeois order, until the course of the revolution had aroused the mass of the nation, peasants and petty bourgeois, standing between the proletariat and the bourgeoisie, against this order, against the rule of capital, and had forced it to attach itself to the proletarians as their protagonists. The workers could buy this victory only through the tremendous defeat in June.

The Class Struggles in France, 1848–50. S.W.1., pp. 148–9

[After 1850 Marx recognised that the communists of 1848 had 'jumped the gun'. He spoke now of ten, fifteen or even fifty years. Yet he remained almost incurably optimistic, forecasting revolutionary crises in 1850, 1854, 1856, 1858 and 1873. Even after the defeat of the Commune he bravely insisted that 'It is to force that in due time the workers will have to appeal . . .']

. . . Scientific insight into the inevitable disintegration of the dominant order of society continually proceeding before our eyes and the ever-growing fury into which the masses are lashed by the old ghostly governments, while at the same time the positive development of the means of production advances with gigantic strides – all this is a sufficient guarantee that the moment a real proletarian revolution breaks out the conditions (though these are certain not to be idyllic) of its immediately next *modus operandi* will be in existence.

Marx to F. Domela-Nieuwenhuis, Feb. 22, 1881.   S.C. p. 411

If you look at the last chapter of my *Eighteenth Brumaire*, you will find that I say that the next attempt of the French Revolution will be no longer, as before, to transfer the bureaucratic-military machine from one hand to another, but to *smash* it, and this is the preliminary condition for every real people's revolution on the continent. And this is what our heroic Party comrades in Paris are attempting.* What elasticity, what historical initiative, what a capacity for sacrifice in these Parisians! After six months of hunger and ruin, caused by internal treachery more even than by the external enemy, they rise, beneath Prussian bayonets, as if there had never been a war between France and Germany and the enemy were not still at the gates of Paris! History has no like example of like greatness! If they are defeated only their 'good nature' will be to blame. They should have marched at once on Versailles,† after first Vonoy and then the reactionary section of the Paris National Guard had themselves retreated. They missed their opportunity because of conscientious scruples. They did not want to *start* a *civil war*, as if that mischievous abortion Thiers had not already started the civil war with his attempt to disarm Paris! Second mistake: The Central Committee‡ surrendered its power too soon, to make way for the Commune. Again from a too 'honourable' scrupulosity! However that may be, the present rising in Paris – even if it be crushed by the wolves, swine and vile curs of the old society – is the most glorious deed of our Party since the June insurrection in Paris. Compare these

* Marx refers to the Paris Commune of 1871. Ed.

† The seat of the National Assembly and of Thiers' government. Ed.

‡ The Comité Central des Vingt Arrondissements, set up in September 1870 to administer Paris. Ed.

Parisians, storming heaven, with the slaves to heaven of the German-Prussian Holy Roman Empire, with its posthumous masquerades reeking of the barracks, the Church, cabbage-Junkerdom and above all, of the Philistine.

Marx to L. Kugelmann, April 12, 1871.   S.W.II., p. 463

Wonderful, indeed, was the change the Commune had wrought in Paris! No longer any trace of the meretricious Paris of the Second Empire. No longer was Paris the rendezvous of British landlords, Irish absentees, American ex-slaveholders and shoddy men, Russian ex-serfowners, and Wallachian boyards. No more corpses at the morgue, no nocturnal burglaries, scarcely any robberies; in fact, for the first time since the days of February 1848, the streets of Paris were safe, and that without any police of any kind. 'We', said a member of the Commune, 'hear no longer of assassination, theft and personal assault; it seems indeed as if the police had dragged along with it to Versailles all its Conservative friends'. The *cocottes* had refound the scent of their protectors – the absconding men of family, religion, and, above all, of property. In their stead, the real women of Paris showed again at the surface – heroic, noble, and devoted, like the women of antiquity. Working, thinking, fighting, bleeding Paris – almost forgetful, in its incubation of a new society, of the cannibals at its gates – radiant in the enthusiasm of its historic initiative!

The Civil War in France.   S.W.I. p. 529

[When writing of actual revolutions, Marx discarded all pretensions to scientific impartiality. There was no inconsistency in this; according to Marx, subjective revolutionary passion is at every stage an agent of the historical process. But one is entitled to ask whether in the mind of a single man – Marx's – subjective passion and scientific analysis can at any point be separated entirely.

Here he speaks of Thiers, the man who crushed the Paris Commune.]

. . . A master in small state roguery, a virtuoso in perjury and treason, a craftsman in all the petty stratagems, cunning devices, and base perfidies of parliamentary party-warfare; never scrupling, when out of office, to fan a revolution, and to stifle it in blood when at the helm of the state; with class prejudices standing him in the place of ideas, and vanity in the place of a heart; his private life as infamous as his public life is odious – even now, when playing the part of a French Sulla, he cannot help setting off the abomination of his deeds by the ridicule of his ostentation.

The Civil War in France.   S.W.1, p. 506

D. Communism

[It has often been said that there were three dominant influences in Marx's intellectual development: German philosophy, French socialism and English political economy. There is much truth in this.

Marx knew of the 'utopian' socialists Owen, Fourier and Saint-Simon by way of their writings. Saint-Simon and his followers were particularly influential in Marx's native Rhineland. It was not, however, until he lived in Paris in 1844 that he encountered more active socialists and communists like Cabet, the followers of Blanqui, Proudhon, Weitling and Flora Tristan.

Marx did not believe that communism could be reached either by drawing up blueprints of future utopias or by trying to persuade the upper classes morally and rationally that capitalist society was anachronistic. He insisted that the proletariat would liberate itself by seizing state power and installing its own dictatorship. The phrase 'dictatorship of the proletariat' he first used in 1850, although the situation is anticipated in the *Communist Manifesto*. Clearly Marx favoured centralisation and was impatient with anarchist demands for the immediate abolition of the state. Probably proletarian dictatorship (*Diktatur*) implied a harsher, post-revolutionary concentration of power than mere working-class rule (*Herrschaft*).]

The proletariat will use its political supremacy to wrest, by degrees, all capital from the bourgeoisie, to centralise all instruments of production in the hands of the State, i.e., of the proletariat organised as the ruling class; and to increase the total of productive forces as rapidly as possible.

Of course, in the beginning, this cannot be effected except by means of despotic inroads on the rights of property, and on the conditions of bourgeois production; by means of measures, therefore, which appear economically insufficient and untenable, but which, in the course of the movement, outstrip themselves, necessitate further inroads upon the old social order, and are unavoidable as a means of entirely revolutionising the mode of production.

These measures will of course be different in different countries.

Nevertheless in the most advanced countries, the following will be pretty generally applicable.

1. Abolition of property in land and application of all rents of land to public purposes.

2. A heavy progressive or graduated income tax.

3. Abolition of all right of inheritance.

4. Confiscation of the property of all emigrants and rebels.

5. Centralisation of credit in the hands of the State, by means of a national bank with State capital and an exclusive monopoly.

6. Centralisation of the means of communication and transport in the hands of the State.

7. Extension of factories and instruments of production owned by the State; the bringing into cultivation of wastelands, and the improvement of the soil generally in accordance with a common plan.

8. Equal liability of all to labour. Establishment of industrial armies, especially for agriculture.

9. Combination of agriculture with manufacturing industries; gradual abolition of the distinction between town and country, by a more equable distribution of the population over the country.

10. Free education for all children in public schools. Abolition of children's factory labour in its present form. Combination of education with industrial production, &c., &c.

When, in the course of development, class distinctions have disappeared, and all production has been concentrated in the hands of a vast association of the whole nation, the public power will lose its political character. Political power, properly so called, is merely the organised power of one class for oppressing another. If the proletariat during its contest with the bourgeoisie is compelled, by the force of circumstances, to organise itself as a class, if, by means of a revolution, it makes itself the ruling class, and, as such, sweeps away by force the old conditions of production, then it will, along with these conditions, have swept away the conditions for the existence of class antagonisms and of classes generally, and will thereby have abolished its own supremacy as a class.

In place of the old bourgeois society, with its classes and class antagonisms, we shall have an association, in which the free development of each is the condition for the free development of all.

C.M., pp. 83–85

. . . Bakunin* maintains that it is the *state* which has created capital, that the capitalist has his capital *only by the grace of the state*.† As, therefore, the state is the chief evil, it is above all the state which must be done away with and then capitalism will go to blazes of itself. We, on the contrary, say: Do away with capital, the concentration of all means of production in the hands of the few, and the state will fall of itself. The difference is an essential one: Without a previous social revolution the abolition of the state is nonsense; the abolition of capital *is* precisely the social revolution and involves a change in the whole mode of production. Now then, inasmuch as to Bakunin the state is the main evil, nothing must be done which can maintain the existence of the state, that is, of any state, whether it be a republic, a monarchy or anything else. Hence *complete abstention from all politics.* To commit a political act, and especially to take part in an election, would be a betrayal of principle. The thing to do is to carry on propaganda, heap abuse upon the state, organise, and when ALL the workers are won over, that is, the majority, depose all the authorities, abolish the state and replace it by the organisation of the International. This great act, with which the millennium begins, is called *social liquidation.*

Now, as the International, according to Bakunin, was not formed for political struggle but in order that it may at once

* The Russian anarchist revolutionary, who challenged the Marxist trend in the First International after 1868. Ed.

† This letter was written by Engels, but is included because of its clear exposition of the Marxist standpoint. Ed.

replace the old state organisation as soon as social liquidation takes place, it follows that it must come as near as possible to the Bakuninist ideal of the society of the future. In this society there will above all be no *authority*, for authority = state = an absolute evil. (Indeed, how these people propose to run a factory, operate a railway or steer a ship without having in the last resort one deciding will, without single management, they of course do not tell us.) The authority of the majority over the minority also ceases. Every individual and every community is autonomous; but as to how a society, even of only two people, is possible unless each gives up some of his autonomy, Bakunin again maintains silence.

Engels to T. Cuno, Jan. 24, 1872.   S.W.II., pp. 468–9

[The Paris Commune, elected in March 1871, was the last revolutionary government to take power in France. Marx championed it. Engels later described it, rashly, as 'the dictatorship of the proletariat'. Although about a third of its members were adherents of the First International, it was neither proletarian in content nor Marxist in ideology. Diverse elements – Jacobin, Blanquist, Proudhonist – fused. The anarchists were no doubt behind the Commune's decree abolishing the centralised French state and establishing autonomous communes throughout France. This was quite contrary to the emphasis of the *Communist Manifesto* and to Marx's *Address to the Central Committee of the Communist League* (1850), in which he and Engels called for the determined centralisation of power by the proletariat and an end to misguided democratic talk about freedom of local self-government. Yet Marx justified the decentralising tendency of the Paris Commune. Later, in 1881, he reflected that the Commune had in no way been socialist. Engels admitted that Marx had in the heat of the struggle] exaggerated the consciously socialist aspects of the Commune.]

The direct antithesis to the empire was the Commune. The cry of 'social republic', with which the revolution of February* was ushered in by the Paris proletariat, did but express a vague

* 1848. Ed.

aspiration after a Republic that was not only to supersede the monarchical form of class-rule, but class-rule itself. The Commune was the positive form of that Republic.

Paris, the central seat of the old governmental power, and, at the same time, the social stronghold of the French working class, had risen in arms against the attempt of Thiers, and the Rurals to restore and perpetuate that old governmental power bequeathed to them by the empire. Paris could resist only because, in consequence of the siege, it had got rid of the army, and replaced it by a National Guard, the bulk of which consisted of working men. This fact was now to be transformed into an institution. The first decree of the Commune, therefore, was the suppression of the standing army, and the substitution for it of the armed people.

The Commune was formed of the municipal councillors, chosen by universal suffrage in the various wards of the town, responsible and revocable at short terms. The majority of its members were naturally working men, or acknowledged representatives of the working class. The Commune was to be a working, not a parliamentary, body, executive and legislative at the same time. Instead of continuing to be the agent of the Central Government, the police was at once stripped of its political attributes, and turned into the responsible and at all times revocable agent of the Commune. So were the officials of all other branches of the Administration. From the members of the Commune downwards, the public service had to be done at *workmen's wages*. The vested interests and the representation allowances of the high dignitaries of State disappeared along with the high dignitaries themselves. Public functions ceased to be the private property of the tools of the Central Government. Not only municipal administration, but the whole initiative hitherto exercised by the State was laid into the hands of the Commune.

The Civil War in France.   S.W.1, pp. 518–19

The Paris Commune was, of course, to serve as a model to all the great industrial centres of France. The communal *régime* once established in Paris and the secondary centres, the old centralised Government would in the provinces, too, have to give way to the self-government of the producers. In a rough sketch of national organisation which the Commune had no time to develop, it states clearly that the Commune was to be the political form of even the smallest country hamlet, and that in the rural districts the standing army was to be replaced by a national militia, with an extremely short term of service. The rural communes of every district were to administer their common affairs by an assembly of delegates in the central town, and these district assemblies were again to send deputies to the National Delegation in Paris, each delegate to be at any time revocable and bound by the *mandat impératif* (formal instructions) of his constituents. The few but important functions which still would remain for a central government were not to be suppressed, as has been intentionally mis-stated, but were to be discharged by Communal, and therefore strictly responsible agents. The unity of the nation was not to be broken, but, on the contrary, to be organised by the Communal Constitution and to become a reality by the destruction of the State power which claimed to be the embodiment of that unity independent of, and superior to, the nation itself, from which it was but a parasitic excrescence. While the merely repressive organs of the old governmental power were to be amputated, its legitimate functions were to be wrested from an authority usurping preeminence over society itself, and restored to the responsible agents of society. Instead of deciding once in three or six years which member of the ruling class was to misrepresent the people in Parliament, universal suffrage was to serve the people, constituted in Communes, as individual suffrage serves every other employer in the search for the workmen and managers in his business. And it is well known that companies, like individuals, in matters of real business generally know how to put the right man in the right place, and, if they for once make a mistake, to redress it promptly. On the other hand, nothing could be more foreign to the spirit of the Commune than to supersede universal suffrage by hierarchic investiture.

The Civil War in France.   S.W.i., pp. 520–1

If the Commune was thus the true representative of all the healthy elements of French society, and therefore the truly national Government, it was, at the same time, as a working men's Government, as the bold champion of the emancipation of labour, emphatically international. Within sight of the Prussian army, that had annexed to Germany two French provinces, the Commune annexed to France the working people all over the world.

The Second Empire had been the jubilee of cosmopolitan black-legism, the rakes of all countries rushing in at its call for a share in its orgies and in the plunder of the French people. Even at this moment the right hand of Thiers is Ganesco, the foul Wallachian, and his left hand is Markovsky, the Russian spy. The Commune admitted all foreigners to the honour of dying for an immortal cause. Between the foreign war lost by their treason, and the civil war fomented by their conspiracy with the foreign invader, the bourgeoisie had found the time to display their patriotism by organising police-hunts upon the Germans in France. The Commune made a German working man its Minister of Labour. Theirs, the bourgeoisie, the Second Empire, had continually deluded Poland by loud professions of sympathy, while in reality betraying her to, and doing the dirty work of, Russia. The Commune honoured the heroic sons of Poland by placing them at the head of the defenders of Paris. And, to broadly mark the new era of history it was conscious of initiating, under the eyes of the conquering Prussians, on the one side, and of the Bonapartist army, led by Bonapartist generals, on the other, the Commune pulled down that colossal symbol of martial glory, the Vendôme column.

The Civil War in France.   S.W.I., pp.526–7

[Marx's early writings reflect the philosophical basis of his interest in communism. He saw it as the culmination of a dialectical process whereby man transcends his own alienation in class society, and then enters a realm of spontaneous co-operation and conscious self-determination. Man becomes 'truly human'.]

But since for the socialist man the *entire so-called history of the world* is nothing but the begetting of man through human labour, nothing but the coming-to-be of nature for man, he has the visible, irrefutable proof of his *birth* through himself, of his *process of coming-to-be*. Since the *real existence* of man and nature has become practical, sensuous and perceptible – since man has become for man as the being of nature, and nature for man as the being of man – the question about an *alien* being, about a being above nature and man – a question which implies the admission of the inessentiality of nature and of man – has become impossible in practice. *Atheism*, as the denial of this inessentiality, has no longer any meaning, for atheism is a *negation of God*, and postulates the *existence of man* through this negation; but socialism as socialism no longer stands in any need of such a mediation. It proceeds from the *practically and theoretically sensuous consciousness* of man and of nature as the *essence*. Socialism is man's *positive self-consciousness*, no longer mediated through the annulment of religion, just as *real life* is man's positive reality, no longer mediated through the annulment of private property, through *communism*. Communism is the position as the negation of the negation, and is hence the *actual* phase necessary for the next stage of historical development in the process of human emancipation and recovery. *Communism* is the necessary pattern and the dynamic principle of the immediate future, but communism as such is not the goal of human development – the structure of human society.

E.P.M., pp. 113–14

Communism is for us not a stable state which is to be established, an *ideal* to which reality will have to adjust itself. We call communism the *real* movement which abolishes the present state of things. The conditions of this movement result from the premises now in existence. . . .   G.I., p. 26

Does this mean that after the fall of the old society there will be a new class domination culminating in a new political power? No.

The condition for the emancipation of the working class is

the abolition of every class, just as the condition for the liberation of the third estate, of the bourgeois order, was the abolition
of all estates and all orders.

The working class, in the course of its development, will
substitute for the old civil society an association which will
exclude classes and their antagonism, and there will be no
more political power properly so-called, since political power
is precisely the official expression of antagonism in civil society.

P.P., p. 174

... But it is just as empirically established that, by the overthrow
of the existing state of society by the communist revolution (of
which more below) and the abolition of private property which
is identical with it, this power, which so baffles the German
theoreticians, will be dissolved; and that then the liberation of
each single individual will be accomplished in the measure in
which history becomes transformed into world-history. From
the above it is clear that the real intellectual wealth of the
individual depends entirely on the wealth of his real connections.
Only then will the separate individuals be liberated from the
various national and local barriers, be brought into practical
connection with the material and intellectual production of the
whole world and be put in a position to acquire the capacity to
enjoy this all-sided production of the whole earth (the creations
of man). Universal dependence, this natural form of the world-
historical co-operation of individuals, will be transformed by
this communist revolution into the control and conscious mastery
of these powers, which, born of the action of men on one another,
have till now overawed and governed men as powers completely
alien to them. ...

G.I., pp. 27–28

[In the early writings Marx discusses the socialist and communist theorists who had preceded him and beyond whose
conceptions he was advancing. The early 'crude communism'
to which he refers is early communist theory rather than a
stage in the development of society. He believed that early
communist writers, unable to eradicate the property mentality
entirely, had merely universalised it.

Marx denounced the contemporary family as a bourgeois institution (although his own family life was strictly conventional). The challenge to the family laid down in the *Communist Manifesto* exercised a horrifying fascination for the bourgeoisie, until Soviet practice and attitudes finally laid these fears to rest.]

. . . Finally, *communism* is the *positive* expression of annulled private property – at first as *universal* private property. By embracing this relation as a *whole*, communism is:

(1) In its first form only a *generalisation* and *consummation* of this relationship. It shows itself as such in a twofold form; on the one hand, the dominion of *material* property bulks so large that it wants to destroy *everything* which is not capable of being possessed by all as *private property*. It wants to abstract by *force* from talent, etc. For it the sole purpose of life and existence is direct, physical *possession*. The category of *labourer* is not done away with, but extended to all men. The relationship of private property persists as the relationship of the community to the world of things. Finally, this movement of counter-posing universal private property to private property finds expression in the bestial form of counterposing to *marriage* (certainly a *form of exclusive private property*) the *community of women*, in which a woman becomes a piece of *communal* and *common* property. It may be said that this idea of the *community* of *women* gives away the *secret* of this as yet completely crude and thoughtless communism. Just as the woman passes from marriage to general prostitution, so the entire world of wealth (that is, of man's objective substance) passes from the relationship of exclusive marriage with the owner of private property to a state of universal prostitution with the community. In negating the *personality* of man in every sphere, this type of communism is really nothing but the logical expression of private property, which is this negation. General *envy* constituting itself as a power is the disguise in which *avarice* re-establishes itself and satisfies itself, only in *another* way. The thoughts of every piece of private property – inherent in each piece as such – are *at least* turned against all *wealthier* private property in the form of envy and the urge to reduce to a common level, so that this

envy and urge even constitute the essence of competition. The crude communism is only the consummation of this envy and of this levelling-down proceeding from the *preconceived* minimum. It has a *definite, limited* standard. How little this annulment of private property is really an appropriation is in fact proved by the abstract negation of the entire world of culture and civilisation, the regression to the *unnatural* simplicity of the *poor and undemanding* man who has not only failed to go beyond private property, but has not yet even attained to it.

The community is only a community of *labour*, and an equality of wages paid out by the communal capital – the *community* as the universal capitalist. Both sides of the relationship are raised to an *imagined* universality – *labour* as a state in which every person is put, and *capital* as the acknowledged universality and power of the community.

. . . The first positive annulment of private property – *crude* communism – is thus merely one *form* in which the vileness of private property, which wants to set itself up as the *positive community, comes to the surface.*

(2) Communism (a) of a political nature still – democratic or despotic; (b) with the annulment of the state, yet still incomplete, and being still affected by private property (i.e. by the estrangement of man). In both forms communism already knows itself to be re-integration or return of man to himself, the transcendence of human self-estrangement; but since it has not yet grasped the positive essence of private property, and just as little the *human* nature of need, it remains captive to it and infected by it. It has, indeed, grasped its concept, but not its essence.

(3) *Communism* as the *positive* transcendence of *private property*, as *human self-estrangement*, and therefore as the real *appropriation of the human* essence by and for man; communism therefore as the complete return of man to himself as a *social* (i.e., human) being – a return become conscious, and accomplished within the entire wealth of previous development. This communism, as fully-developed naturalism, equals humanism, and as fully-developed humanism equals naturalism; it is the *genuine* resolu-

tion of the conflict between man and nature and between man and man – the true resolution of the strife between existence and essence, between objectification and self-confirmation, between freedom and necessity, between the individual and the species. Communism is the riddle of history solved, and it knows itself to be this solution.

E.P.M., pp. 99–102

Abolition of the family! Even the most radical flare up at this infamous proposal of the Communists.

On what foundation is the present family, the bourgeois family, based? On capital, on private gain. In its completely developed form this family exists only among the bourgeoisie. But this state of things finds its complement in the practical absence of the family among the proletarians, and in public prostitution.

The bourgeois family will vanish as a matter of course when its complement vanishes, and both will vanish with the vanishing of capital.

C.M., p. 77

The bourgeois clap-trap about the family and education, about the hallowed co-relation of parent and child, becomes all the more disgusting, the more, by the action of Modern Industry, all family ties among the proletarians are torn asunder, and their children transformed into simple articles of commerce and instruments of labour.

But you Communists would introduce community of women, screams the whole bourgeoisie in chorus.

The bourgeois sees in his wife a mere instrument of production. He hears that the instruments of production are to be exploited in common, and, naturally, can come to no other conclusion than that the lot of being common to all will likewise fall to the women.

He has not even a suspicion that the real point aimed at is to do away with the status of women as mere instruments of production.

For the rest, nothing is more ridiculous than the virtuous indignation of our bourgeois at the community of women which, they pretend, is to be openly and officially established by the Communists. The Communists have no need to introduce community of women; it has existed almost from time immemorial.

Our bourgeois, not content with having the wives and daughters of their proletarians at their disposal, not to speak of common prostitutes, take the greatest pleasure in seducing each other's wives.

Bourgeois marriage is in reality a system of wives in common and thus, at the most, what the Communists might possibly be reproached with, is that they desire to introduce, in substitution for a hypocritically concealed, an openly legalised community of women. For the rest, it is self-evident that the abolition of the present system of production must bring with it the abolition of the community of women springing from that system, i.e., of prostitution both public and private.   C.M., pp. 78–79

['The workers have no country.' This was an article of faith, not a fact. It has remained an article of faith; the nation state, communist or capitalist, lives on.

Marx and Engels were in reality acutely conscious of the nationality question. They regarded the liberation of Poland and Italy, and the unification of Germany, as essential pre-requisites to a European revolution. At the same time they were themselves affected by German nationalism and by a belief in the innate superiority of the Germans to the Slavs.]

The Communists are further reproached with desiring to abolish countries and nationality.

The working men have no country. We cannot take from them what they have not got. Since the proletariat must first of all acquire political supremacy, must rise to be the leading class of the nation, must constitute itself *the* nation, it is, so far, itself national, though not in the bourgeois sense of the word.

National differences and antagonisms between peoples are daily more and more vanishing, owing to the development of the bourgeoisie, to freedom of commerce, to the world market, to uniformity in the mode of production and in the conditions of life corresponding thereto.

The supremacy of the proletariat will cause them to vanish still faster. United action, of the leading civilised countries at least, is one of the first conditions for the emancipation of the proletariat.

In proportion as the exploitation of one individual by another is put an end to, the exploitation of one nation by another will also be put an end to. In proportion as the antagonism between classes within the nation vanishes, the hostility of one nation to another will come to an end.

C.M., pp. 79–80

[Marx believed that the division of labour, the basis of human alienation, would disappear in communist society (although in later years he seems to have been less confident of this). Men would lead a full, creative, human life. The struggle of man against man would give way to a common struggle against nature. Property and money relationships, and the attitudes which sprang from them, would vanish. Needs, not capacities, would determine the system of distribution. 'From each according to his abilities, to each according to his needs.' Such an ideal society would no doubt require high productivity and practically unlimited abundance.]

In this sense, the theory of the Communists may be summed up in the single sentence: Abolition of private property.

C.M., p. 71

. . . For as soon as labour is distributed, each man has a particular, exclusive sphere of activity, which is forced upon him and from which he cannot escape. He is a hunter, a fisherman, a shepherd, or a critical critic, and must remain so if he does not want to lose his means of livelihood; while in communist society, where nobody has one exclusive sphere of activity but each can become accomplished in any branch he wishes, society regulates the general production and thus makes it possible for me to do one thing today and another tomorrow, to hunt in the morning, fish in the afternoon, rear cattle in the evening, criticize after dinner, just as I have a mind, without ever becoming hunter, fisherman, shepherd or critic. G.I., p. 22

In a future society, in which class antagonism will have ceased, in which there will no longer be any classes, use will no longer be determined by the *minimum* time of production; but the time of production devoted to different articles will be determined by the degree of their social utility. P.P., p. 63

. . . But one of the most vital principles of communism, a principle which distinguishes it from all reactionary socialism, is its empiric view, based on a knowledge of men, that differences of brain, of intellectual capacity, do not imply any difference whatsoever in the nature of the stomach and of physical needs; therefore the false tenet, based upon existing circumstances, 'to each according to his capacity', must be changed, in so far as it relates to enjoyment in its narrower sense, into the tenet, 'to each according to his need'; in other words, a different form of activity, of labour, confers no privileges in respect of possession and enjoyment. . . . G.I., pp. 189–90

Let us take first of all the words 'proceeds of labour' in the sense of the product of labour; then the co-operative proceeds of labour from the *total social product*.

From this must now be deducted:

First, cover for replacement of the means of production used up.

Secondly, additional portion for expansion of production.

Thirdly, reserve or insurance funds to provide against accidents, dislocations caused by natural calamities, etc.

These deductions from the 'undiminished proceeds of labour' are an economic necessity and their magnitude is to be determined according to available means and forces, and partly by computation of probabilities, but they are in no way calculable by equity.

There remains the other part of the total product, intended to serve as means of consumption.

Before this is divided among the individuals, there has to be deducted again, from it:

First, the general costs of administration not belonging to production.

This part will, from the outset, be very considerably restricted in comparison with present-day society and it diminishes in proportion as the new society develops.

Secondly, that which is intended for the common satisfaction of needs, such as schools, health services, etc.

From the outset this part grows considerably in comparison with present-day society and it grows in proportion as the new society develops.

Thirdly, funds for those unable to work, etc., in short, for what is included under so-called official poor relief today.

Only now do we come to the 'distribution' which the programme, under Lassallean influence, alone has in view in its narrow fashion, namely, to that part of the means of consumption which is divided among the individual producers of the co-operative society.

The 'undiminished proceeds of labour' have already unnoticeably become converted into the 'diminished' proceeds, although what the producer is deprived of in his capacity as a private individual benefits him directly or indirectly in his capacity as a member of society.

Just as the phrase of the 'undiminished proceeds of labour' has disappeared, so now does the phrase of the 'proceeds of labour' disappear altogether.

Within the co-operative society based on common ownership of the means of production, the producers do not exchange their products; just as little does the labour employed on the products appear here *as the value* of these products, as a material quality possessed by them, since now, in contrast to capitalist society, individual labour no longer exists in an indirect fashion but directly as a component part of the total labour. The phrase 'proceeds of labour', objectionable also today on account of its ambiguity, thus loses all meaning.

What we have to deal with here is a communist society, not as it has *developed* on its own foundations, but, on the contrary, just as it *emerges* from capitalist society; which is thus in every respect, economically, morally and intellectually, still swamped with the birth marks of the old society from whose womb it emerges. Accordingly, the individual producer receives back from society – after the deductions have been made – exactly what he gives to it. What he has given to it is his individual quantum of labour. For example, the social working day consists of the sum of the individual hours of work; the individual labour time of the individual producer is the part of the social working day contributed by him, his share in it. He receives a certificate from society that he has furnished such and such an amount of labour (after deducting his labour for the common funds), and with this certificate he draws from the social stock of means of consumption as much as costs the same amount of labour. The same amount of labour which he has given to society in one form he receives back in another.

Hence, *equal right* here is still in principle – *bourgeois right*, although principle and practice are no longer at loggerheads, while the exchange of equivalents in commodity exchange only exists *on the average* and not in the individual case.

In spite of this advance, this *equal right* is still constantly stigmatised by a bourgeois limitation. The right of the producers is *proportional* to the labour they supply; the equality consists in the fact that measurement is made with an *equal standard*, labour.

But one man is superior to another physically or mentally and so supplies more labour in the same time, or can labour for a longer time; and labour, to serve as a measure, must be defined by its duration or intensity, otherwise it ceases to be a standard of measurement. This *equal* right is an unequal right for unequal labour. It recognises no class differences, because everyone is only a worker like everyone else; but it tacitly recognises unequal individual endowment and thus productive capacity as natural privileges. *It is, therefore, a right of inequality, in its content, like every right.* Right by its very nature can consist only in the application of an equal standard; but unequal individuals (and they would not be different individuals if they were not unequal) are measurable only by an equal standard in so far as they are brought under an equal point of view, are taken from one *definite* side only, for instance, in the present case, are regarded *only* as *workers* and nothing more is seen in them, everything else being ignored. Further, one worker is married, another not; one has more children than another, and so on and so forth. Thus, with an equal performance of labour, and hence an equal share in the social consumption fund, one will in fact receive more than another, one will be richer than another, and so on. To avoid all these defects, right instead of being equal would have to be unequal.

But these defects are inevitable in the first phase of communist society as it is when it has just emerged after prolonged birth pangs from capitalist society. Right can never be higher than the economic structure of society and its cultural development conditioned thereby.

In a higher phase of communist society, after the enslaving subordination of the individual to the division of labour, and therewith also the antithesis between mental and physical labour, has vanished; after labour has become not only a means of life but life's prime want; after the productive forces have also increased with the all-round development of the individual, and all the springs of co-operative wealth flow more abundantly – only then can the narrow horizon of bourgeois right be crossed in its entirety and society inscribe on its banners: From each according to his ability, to each according to his needs!

Critique of the Gotha Programme.   S.W.II., pp. 21–24

Would the state 'wither away' entirely under communism? Engels affirmed that it would, adopting Saint-Simon's formula that the government of people would give way to the administration of things. But Marx was less explicit. In a passage written in 1875, he referred briefly and without further explanation to 'the future state of the communist society'. Unlike the more dogmatic anarchists, he and Engels realised that in a highly complex industrial society some form of authority would remain indispensable. But it might take an entirely voluntary form and not require the legitimisation of formal state⌉ power.

The question then arises: what transformation will the state undergo in communist society? In other words, what social functions will remain in existence there that are analagous to present functions of the state? The question can only be answered scientifically, and one does not get a flea-hop nearer to the problem by a thousandfold combination of the word people with the word state.

Between capitalist and communist society lies the period of the revolutionary transformation of the one into the other. There corresponds to this also a political transition period in which the state can be nothing but *the revolutionary dictatorship of the proletariat*.

Now the programme does not deal with this nor with the future state of communist society.

Critique of the Gotha Programme.   S.W.II., pp. 32–33

Bibliography

The most complete bibliography of the works of Marx is Maximilien Rubel, *Bibliographie des Oeuvres de Karl Marx*. Paris, Rivière. 1956.

In addition to the works of Marx, and the editions of his writings, given in the preface, the following English collected editions are recommended. (All are published by Messrs. Lawrence & Wishart, except where indicated).

K. Marx, *Capital*, Volume II (1885). Edited by F. Engels. Translated with reference to the translation published by Charles H. Kerr & Co., Chicago. London, 1957.

K. Marx and F. Engels, On Britain.

K. Marx and F. Engels, On Colonialism.

K. Marx and F. Engels, The First Indian War of Independence (1857–1859).

K. Marx, *Notes on Indian History*.

K. Marx and F. Engels, *The Civil War in the United States*.

K. Marx, *Theories of Surplus Value*, Part I. Translated by Emile Burns. n.d.

Marx and Engels on Malthus. Translated by D. L. and R. L. Meek. Edited by Ronald L. Meek. 1953.

K. Marx and F. Engels, *The German Ideology*, London. 1965.

Of the writings of Engels, a number of shorter pieces are collected in K. Marx and F. Engels, *Selected Works*, Volume I. Volume II, includes Engels' 'Socialism: Utopian and Scientific' (1876–8), 'The Origin of the Family, Private Property and the State' (1884), 'Ludwig Feuerbach and the End of Classical German Philosophy' (1886), and 'The Peasant Question in France and Germany' (1894).

See also Engels' *Dialectics of Nature*, London, Lawrence & Wishart, 1954, and his *Anti-Dühring* (*Herr Eugene Dühring's Revolution in Science*), London, Lawrence & Wishart, 1960.

Engels' early work, 'The Condition of the Working Class in

England' (1844) is included in the collection *K. Marx and F. Engels, On Britain*, London, Lawrence & Wishart, 1962.

Secondary Works

Of the many works in English devoted to Marx's life and work, the following are particularly recommended. Although their attitudes towards Marx vary considerably, they can all be taken seriously.

Acton, H. B., *The Illusion of an Epoch*, London, Cohen & West, 1955.

Adams, H. P., *Karl Marx in his Earlier Writings*, London, Allen & Unwin, 1940.

Aron, Raymond, *Main Currents in Sociological Thought*, Volume I, translated by Richard Howard and Helen Weaver, London, Weidenfeld, 1965.

Berlin, Isaiah, *Karl Marx*, London, O.U.P., 1963.

Bober, Karl, *Karl Marx's Interpretation of History*, Cambridge, Mass., Harvard U.P., 1950.

Bottomore, T. B. and Rubel, Maximilien, *Introduction to Karl Marx. Selected Writings in Sociology and Social Philosophy*, London, Penguin, 1963.

Carr, E. H., *Karl Marx: A Study in Fanaticism*, London, J. M. Dent & Sons, 1934.

Cole, G. D. H., *A History of Socialist Thought*, Volume II, *Marxism and Anarchism (1850–90)*, London, Macmillan, 1954.

Collins, Henry and Abramsky, Chaim, *Karl Marx and the English Labour Movement*, London, Macmillan, 1965.

Hobsbawm, Eric, Introduction to Karl Marx, *Pre-Capitalist Economic Formations*, London, Lawrence & Wishart, 1964.

Hook, Sidney, *From Hegel to Marx*, Michigan, Ann Arbor, 1962.

Kamenka, Eugene, *The Ethical Foundations of Marxism*, London, Routledge & Kegan Paul, 1962.

Lewis, John, *The Life and Teaching of Karl Marx*, London, Lawrence & Wishart, 1965.

Lichteim, George, *Marxism*, London, Routledge & Kegan Paul, 1961.

Lindsay, A. D., *Karl Marx's Capital: an Introductory Essay*, London, Cumberlege, 1947.

MacIntyre, Alasdair C., *Marxism, an Interpretation*, London, S.C.M. Press, 1953.

Marcuse, Herbert, *Reason and Revolution: Hegel and the Rise of Social Theory*, New York, The Humanities Press, 1954.

Mehring, Franz, *Karl Marx: The Story of his Life*, London, John Lane the Bodley Head, 1936.

Meyer, Alfred G., *Marxism the Union of Theory and Practice*, Cambridge, Mass., Harvard U.P., 1954.

Mitrany, David, *Marx against the Peasant*, London, Weidenfeld, 1951.

Ossowski, Stanislaw, *Class Structure in the Social Consciousness*, Translated by Sheila Patterson, London, Routledge & Kegan Paul, 1963.

Plamenatz, John, *German Marxism and Russian Communism*, London, Longmans, 1954.

Plamenatz, John, *Man and Society*, Volume II. London, Longmans, 1963.

Schlesinger, Rudolf, *Marx, His Time and Ours*, London, Routledge & Kegan Paul, 1950.

Schumpeter, J. A., *Capitalism, Socialism and Democracy*, London, Allen & Unwin, 1943.

Sweezy, Paul, *The Theory of Capitalist Development: Principles of Marxian Political Economy*, New York, O.U.P., 1942.

Talmon, J. L., *Political Messianism, the Romantic Phase*, London, Secker & Warburg, 1960.

Tucker, Robert C., *Philosophy and Myth in Karl Marx*, Cambridge, Cambridge U.P., 1961.

Ulam, Adam B., *The Unfinished Revolution*, New York, Random House, 1960.

Wetter, Gustav A., *Dialectical Materialism*, Translated by Peter Heath, London, Routledge, 1958.

Wilson, Edmund, *To the Finland Station*, London, W. H. Allen, 1940.

Wolfe, Bertram, *Marxism*, New York, Dial Press, 1965.

Index